LEGACY OF

LEADERSHIP

- VOLUME 1 -

LEGACY OF LEADERSHIP

- VOLUME 1 -

STORIES AND STRATEGIES TO IMPROVE YOUR CRISIS LEADERSHIP

BY

MIKE MCKENNA

MARTY-
THANK YOU
for your
contribution, your
Leadership + your
LEGACY!
Mike.

Mike McKenna/TEAM Solutions

Visit my website at TEAM-Solutions.US

Visit the book's website at LegacyOfLeadership.US

Printed in the United States of America

ISBN: 9781704786292

DEDICATION

I dedicate this book to my children, Ethan and Emily.

Their eventual success as a leader of themselves and others is my greatest legacy.

~ Mike

The legacy of heroes is the memory of a great name and the inheritance of a great example.

~ Benjamin Disraeli

What we do in life echoes in eternity.

~ Maximus Decimus Meridius (from the movie, "Gladiator")

The things you do for yourself are gone when you are gone, but the things you do for others remain as your legacy.

~Kalu Ndukwe Kalu

TABLE OF CONTENTS

FOREWORD

It is a privilege to be writing this foreword for Mike McKenna. Not only do I respect him as a professional, but I am glad to call him my friend. We met as fellow instructors somewhat late in my career, just over four years ago. As instructors for our nation's responders in a world-class training agency, our job is not so much to simply teach, but is better described as "facilitating the learning process." I have had the pleasure to stand side by side with Mike during many of these rather intense training moments, and if we are to measure his success as an instructor by how much is learned, then Mike can only be described as a master.

Like many of the interviewees who make up the chapters in this book, it was my honor to serve with a major fire department for over thirty years. As both an instructor and responder, I have had the pleasure of working alongside many of these same people whose stories are included in this book. While their stories are not polished, their words are sincere, and their experience is real. In discussing their viewpoints on effective crisis leadership, you will see recurring themes of courage, compassion, communication, and simply stepping forward in a moment of need. You will be reminded of the importance of being well trained, and of being able to demonstrate the technical competence that comes from education, experience, and time. You will understand that they were effective leaders in their daily lives, and on a day of crisis they stepped forward and people listened and followed. As you read their stories, it is unlikely that you will be surprised by what effective crisis leadership requires in the real world; no doubt you have seen it in your own life experience.

In preparation for writing this foreword, I wanted to understand Mike's motivation for writing this book. He and I agreed to talk after I completed reading it. After reading it, I realized there was no need to ask. His mission was clear. Our nation has a continued need for response professionals to react with purpose and integrity at times of crisis, and therein lies the necessity for effective leadership. This book is another one of Mike's tools to guide you, the reader, to your own lessons learned. I encourage you to read this book with the understanding that you are listening to the experiences of leaders just like yourself, who have lived through decades of incidents that went well, and some that did not. You will be reminded that on most days there is no simple and clear path to success during a crisis, but nonetheless, there is a going forward. And if on that day you are willing to simply stand up, bring your voice and experience to the incident management process, then you can and will play an instrumental role in helping your community, just like the people who shared their stories in this book.

Enjoy the read. I know I did.

Mike A.

ACKNOWLEDGMENTS

Some key folks helped fuel this mini-tome.

John James (interviewed herein) was the person who suggested that I write a second book, including some examples of people using the lessons I taught in my first book. While the focus shifted a little by the time I published this, John's initial nudge was instrumental to me deciding to start this book project.

Finishing the book required different inspirations.

It didn't take long to see that what started as a writing project was developing into a service project. A clear image developed in my mind of emerging leaders consuming this book and becoming a better leader as a result. Acknowledging the responsibility to serve and support them by sharing these stories was instrumental in bringing this project to fruition.

When I pondered the deep-seated relationship between *leadership* and *legacy*, asking Mike A. to write the foreword was the most logical choice since he epitomizes both. He sets the standard for effective leadership but also has a long legacy of leaders who credit him for contributing to their growth. I'm one of them.

This interview project also creates a reference where my children can read the stories of my personal heroes. The opportunity to provide this for them helped me to understand the impact this project can have.

My parents, each in their own way, have always encouraged me to "improve the breed" and to strive for what is just out of reach. I hope to carry that torch of responsibility with distinction.

My wife Tonya's unwavering support for my occasional early mornings, late nights, and mental vacancy is my greatest fuel. Thank you for everything, Tonya.

And lastly, a heartfelt thanks go to the men and women who agreed to an interview for this project. There was a 'leap of faith' element to this project, and their support and patience with me were essential success factors.

I'm eternally grateful to them.

INTRODUCTION

After I wrote my first book, "The Response Leadership Sequence," one of the people who read it and liked it suggested a follow-up. His idea for me was to bring some of the stories to life by collecting experiences from responders on how they worked their way through a crisis response.

Flattered and intrigued, but mostly reluctant. While I was still coming to terms with the reality that I had written one book, it seemed so far away that I would actually write a second book.

So, I sat on the idea. For almost a year.

When my travel started to abate in the late fall, I decided that if I was going to honor that request and bring some of the outstanding people and crisis stories together, that it wouldn't write itself.

While flying home from a business trip, I brainstormed a list of people who I felt had some inspirational and instructional crisis leadership stories to share and the five questions that I'd like to ask them.

Those five questions all centered around crisis leadership and gratefully, almost everyone I contacted agreed to participate in one form or another.

WHO IS INCLUDED? AND WHY?

So, who did I ask to participate, and why?

Below are some criteria I used:

1) Leadership experience, obviously.

Most of them are retired or late in their careers. For better or worse, their lessons and the scars are theirs, learned from their firsthand experiences as a leader during crises.

Some of them I've known for a while and have experienced their leadership first hand.

Some I've grown to know through other projects, joint experiences, or a common network.

2) Growth mindset

In my first book, I addressed the differences between a mindset that is dynamic and growth-oriented versus one that is more fixed and comfortable.

There are some very competent folks I know who have reached a place in their lives where continued growth is not a priority. I've discovered that a fixed mindset also makes it harder to recognize and encourage growth in others, so I chose to exclude them.

Crises don't discriminate, so I sought out folks from different places and job sectors to optimize the variety of perspectives.

3) Diversity of discipline

From the *public sector*, perspectives include those from:

- ✓ Fire
- ✓ Elected Officials
- ✓ EMS
- ✓ Military
- ✓ Law
- ✓ Emergency Mgmt.

From the *private sector*, perspectives include those from:

- ✓ Transportation (aviation and rail)
- ✓ Finance
- ✓ Project Management
- ✓ Academia
- ✓ Management Consulting
- ✓ Entrepreneurialism
- ✓ Private Investigations
- ✓ Non-Profit Organizations
- ✓ Corporate Security

- ✓ Healthcare
- ✓ Communications

4) Diversity of geographic location

Every region of the United States is represented, from 'sea to shining sea,' including the following states:

- ✓ Washington
- ✓ California
- ✓ Colorado
- ✓ Texas
- ✓ Kansas
- ✓ Illinois
- ✓ Ohio
- ✓ Alabama
- ✓ North Carolina
- ✓ New York
- ✓ Massachusetts

Even Iraq, by way of Texas, is represented.

HOW TO USE THIS BOOK

On a superficial level, this is a book of interviews. However, to gain the full benefit of the content, I encourage you to look deep within each interviewer's words for the depth of knowledge they bring to crisis leadership.

This book is not sequential, so you can freely jump between chapters.

Each chapter focuses on just one interviewee. If you know any of them, their chapter may be a good place to start.

A biographical snapshot starts each chapter, including a photo of the leader, relevant job and location information, a quote that I attribute to them, and for most of them, their contact information.

If you like what they have to say, consider reaching out to share with them how you benefited from their stories.

At the beginning of each chapter, I offer some background on the person, and I offer my opinion as to why I believe they're a crisis leader.

Every person answered the same five questions, their answers recorded.

1) *What is a Crisis Leader?*
2) *Please share an example when you relied on your crisis leadership?*
3) *What do you know now that you wish you knew then?*

4) *What advice would you give someone who wants to improve their crisis leadership?*

5) *Who is a crisis leader that influenced your career?*

The recordings were professionally transcribed to bring their stories to a readable form.

Have your words ever been transcribed? Without the nuances present in face-to-face verbal communication, the results can be startling.

No matter how literate and conversant we are in real-life, verbatim transcripts tend to come out cumbersome, folksy … yet still authentic.

The interview's authenticity is critical, so very little of the person's response was changed. Mild edits are my attempt to provide clarity to each person's message.

Grammar Nazis, consider yourselves warned.

To immerse yourself in each person's stories, look at their picture, read their brief bio, and then read their words as if they were sitting across the table from you.

You'll see some emphasis added to some words and passages. Any emphasis you see is mine and simply reflects my interpretation of what I think represents the core message or something that merits special attention.

These interviews capture so much more than stories.

They pack actionable lessons learned over a career of crisis leadership that we can all use.

That's why the ultimate value of these interviews lies with you, the reader.

How will you apply what you hear to add to your leadership journey?

KEY TAKEAWAYS

To help pave that journey, at the end of each interview, I include the Key Takeaways that I gleaned from listening to the interview.

- At the end of the book, I share a link where to download a complete list of my Key Takeaways and other helpful analytics.

It's important to note here that a Key Takeaway for me won't always be a Key Takeaway for you.

Therefore, I strongly encourage you to highlight, bookmark and add your preferred emphasis to the passages that are the most meaningful to you for your situation.

At the end of the book, I share how to view and listen to each of the recorded interviews, easily download and print the Key Takeaways, and access other helpful analytics.

LEGACY

As I listened to each of these interviewees, two persistent thoughts ran through my head:

1) I wish I had access to their leadership wisdom when I was younger.
2) Am I doing enough to share these enduring lessons so that they will be accessible and memorable for future generations?

We are all new at our craft initially, so this project intends to help fill the knowledge gap for emerging leaders.

And the selfless service, the enduring lessons, and the legacy of leadership in the following pages are certainly worth remembering.

Pep Guardiola is a professional soccer (fútbol) manager, tactician, and svengali. He's currently at the helm of one of the top teams in England's top-level Premier League. Back in 2008, he brought his innovative soccer approach to FC Barcelona, in Spain's top La Liga (league).

While at FC Barcelona, he led his side to an unprecedented streak of 14 trophies from commanding victories against Europe's strongest teams. His achievements are considered some of the greatest successes in soccer history.

Guardiola's leadership of FC Barcelona during those years molded a team that is frequently mentioned as the greatest team to lace up a pair of cleats.

Pep's response when asked about this 'legado' (legacy):

> "I'm often asked if it was the greatest team ever. Or one of the greatest. And it's a question that doesn't have an answer.
>
> It's like a new book that's published, is it good or not?
>
> Or a new film that premiers, is it any good? We'll know the answer in 25 years; it depends if people are still talking about us.
>
> If after 25 years we're still talking about a book that's because it's good.

If we're still watching a film in 25 years' time, it must be good.

The same will happen with our team.

But were we better than Sacchi's Milan or Pele's Brazil, or Johan's Ajax?

Everyone will have their opinion, which they'll defend passionately.

I would tell you that my team was brilliant, but Johan would argue that his team was better.

And Arrigo Sacchi would say the same about his Milan side. And we'd all be in the right.

But if they remember us in 25 years' time, they won't talk about the titles we won they'll talk about how we played.

If they remember us, it's because they enjoyed watching us.

But that's the big mystery, will we be remembered or not?"

+++

xxx

In the speed of life, the memorable experiences we seek are often buried under distracting memes, half-witted bumper-sticker logic, and savvy marketing hucksters promising leadership mastery, etc.

Bright, shiny, and omnipresent one minute … relegated to the dustbin of history the next minute.

My mission, including this book, aims to improve those outcomes. Leaving a worthwhile legacy is worth more than money, a trinket, or a title.

A legacy is the highest form of remembrance because it has the potential to connect our emotions, our brain, and our capability to improve at something.

In a world starving for capable leaders, a legacy of leadership provides us the blueprint to build great things for ourselves and for those we serve.

Let's begin.

ALLEN OWEN – MAYOR OF MISSOURI CITY, TX

Home	Missouri City, Texas
Then	Mayor of Missouri City, Texas
Now	Consultant
Contact	**LinkedIn:** mayor-allen-owen-28891a89/
Quote	*"Depend on those who have been there ..."*

WHY ALLEN IS A CRISIS LEADER

I met Allen through a mutual friend. 'If I want to interview a real crisis leader, you have to talk with Allen Owen,' I was told.

Now, after having the pleasure of interviewing him, I completely understand. Allen Owen served as Mayor of Missouri City, Texas when two catastrophic hurricanes came through. Not one, but two.

Unlike elected officials that left their citizens leaderless during a crisis, Mayor Owen stayed and led his citizens through to the sunny side of two disasters.

His leadership during a crisis is self-evident, and his stories about his innovative solutions are harrowing and inspiring.

#1 - WHAT IS A CRISIS LEADER?

All right, good morning Mike, thanks for asking me for the interview. I think the first question that you posed to us was, what is your definition of a crisis leader.

And I think, first off, a crisis is defined at the time when a difficult decision must be made, in a time of intense difficulty, trouble, and danger.

And a crisis leader I think is one who accepts that responsibility, and is not afraid to make those tough decisions for the safety and the well-being of everyone he's responsible to and for. And it's not an easy thing to be a decision-maker in difficult times, but that's what they pay us the big bucks for.

#2 - PLEASE SHARE AN EXAMPLE WHEN YOU RELIED ON YOUR CRISIS LEADERSHIP?

I look at two major events, and I've been through eight major events in my years, 24 years as mayor, but during Ike, during Hurricane Ike, and during Harvey are two that I would talk about the most.

I guess during Ike, and let me just say, that Ike was all wind and no rain. Harvey was all rain and no wind.

So during Ike, we lost electricity. And we were without electricity for anywhere from five to 10 days. I was without electricity in my own house for ten days. But a gasoline station shut down. They didn't have electricity to pump gas, and those few that did had long lines.

And I'm sitting in line one day getting gas for my generator, and I look across the street, and the Chevron station had the lights on, but they were boarded up. So I knew they had electricity. So I went back to our Emergency Operation Center, and I got the telephone number of the owner of the station.

And I called the owner, and I said, "You have electricity at your station?"

"Yes, sir."

I said, "Do you have gasoline in your tanks?"

"Yes, sir."

I said, " I'm gonna give you two choices. "You can open your station or I'm gonna open it for ya."

He said, "What do you mean?"

I said, "I'm gonna cut the locks off your door."

I said, "I got people waiting in line "and you've got gas in the ground. "And you've got electricity."

"I don't have anybody to run it."

I said, "I do. "I have a friend who owns C-stores. He's well capable of running your service station."

So I said, "When can you be here?"

"Well, I can be there in the morinin."

I said, "Fine." "I'll meet you in the morning."

So I met him that morning. He opened the station. My friend opened the gas pumps, and we started pumping gas to people.

I had city employees who were literally pumping gas — having fun. They were checking oil. They were doing all the fun things that you used to do at a service station.

But the main reason I had it was is that my people, they were going to and from home, needed gas to get to and from the EOC (Emergency Operations Center) and they didn't have it either.

So I opened up that station on one side of it for city employees to come and get gas.

Now we paid for it. The pumps would take credit cards, but they couldn't take cash. And it's kind of ironic that the Exxon station across the street opened up after we did and their gas was 2 cents higher than what the Chevron station was. I started a gas war. [laughter]

But, you know, people said, "How did you do that?"

I said, "Well, the governor gave me that power." You know to confiscate and to take things that are necessary. There was food. There was ice. There was a lot of stuff in that convenience store. And we had people come into the police station looking for food for kids and stuff. And I said, "Come down here." I said, "The guy doesn't want this stuff anymore. "It's gonna spoil if somebody doesn't come get it."

So we even gave the food away that was in the store. The ice that was still in the ice machines that were there. Milk. All that kind of stuff.

And that was a decision that a lot of people, I have a Congressman that loves telling that story in Congress.

That I've got a mayor that confiscated a gas station.

But that's a decision that I felt was in the best interest of the citizens, and it was a decision that the governor gives us the ability to do. And once you declare that declaration, that emergency declaration, you have that power.

During Harvey was a little bit different.

As I said, Harvey was all rain and no wind. We never lost power, but we had 18 and 20 inches of rain. So we had severe flooding.

And during that time, I had 57 state troopers and 17 National Guardsmen who came to Missouri City to start helping will patrolling the streets and doing high water rescues.

And they came unprepared to stay. And I have a City Center outside a golf course. Obviously, we weren't playing golf. And I said, "Look, guys, "you're not gonna stay in your cars. "I've got a big building over here. "I've got electricity. "I've got a kitchen in it. "It's not being used. So I housed those state troopers and those National Guardsmen for about a week while they were here. And they patrolled the streets and did the high water rescues.

But I didn't have everything I needed.

They came here not prepared to stay. So they didn't have bedding. They didn't have the essentials that were needed. Personal items.

So these big stores have what's called Knox Boxes on the outside of them. The little red box on the outside of the door has a key to the front door in it that the firemen can use to go in it.

And I had a good friend who was head of security for H-E-B (grocery store) and Academy (sporting goods). And I called them both, and I said, "Guys, when your alarm goes off in your stores, "don't be alarmed." I said, "We're going into your stores, and we're gonna take things that are necessary for us to do these high water rescues."

We went into Academy and took kayaks, rope, waders, boots. Everything that we could find in Academy that we needed to help our firefighters and patrolmen.

We went into H-E-B, took food. We went into Walmart. We took air mattresses, sheets, personal hygiene equipment. And supplied those guys while they were here.

Again, everybody said, "Well, how did you do that?"

I said, " Well, the governor gave me the ability "to confiscate what I needed."

Now, we went back to Academy and said, "Look, here's what we took." Because to get reimbursed from FEMA, we have to itemize everything that you do take.

Like I said, the gasoline we paid for. And by the way, the guy was bringing more gas. Wanted my people to pump gas. I finally said, "No, no, no, no, no. "You need to pump your own gas now."

Anyway, went to Academy, and I gave 'em $25,000 for the stuff. Guy said it was the best sales day he'd had in a long time.

We went to Walmart and H-E-B, and they both said, "We don't want any money. "It's yours. "Take whatever you wanted, and we don't want a reimbursement." Again, those are decisions that, you know, those are personal decisions.

I could have sat there in both of those situations and not done anything. But as an EOC coordinator and as a person *who really wants to believe in taking care of his people, I made those hard decisions.*

And it's not easy to make those decisions.

Some might say, "Well, did they not want you "going in those stores?" I said, "Well, they didn't have a choice."

They knew that I could go in whether they wanted to or not. I think those are the things.

Those are probably the best two examples that I use, and other people use to talk about with me is. You know, I even got accused of stealing. [laughter] Some of my critics said I was stealing. I said, "Well, you don't know what you're talking about." But I said, "I called 'em all before I went in."

Anyway, those are the two examples that I would use.

Well, when the Brazos River was flooding.

And we were flying a drone. We'd fly drones up and down these levees looking for different issues, and they called me one afternoon and said, "Mayor, we have a problem.

"One of the big levees has about a 100-yard section that is sloughing." And I'm going, "Whoa."

This is major because before that levee was built, had it not been built, there were about 15,000 homes that were at risk of being flooded. And it had that levee breached, but anyway, I'm flying this and I'm trying to keep an eye on it, and all of a sudden my people tell me that the FAA grounded my drone.

They didn't want the drones up flying around because of the helicopters and news people. And so, Congressman Pete Olson had been coming by the Emergency Operations Center almost on a daily basis. And I think Pete probably serves on a FAA committee or whatever it is.

I called Pete, and I said, "Pete, I have a problem."

I said, "The FAA has grounded my drone."

And I said, "We have a situation on the levee."

I said, "It's sloughing away."

In about 15 minutes, the guys came in and said, "Sir, the FAA has lifted the restriction. "We can fly again."

I said, "Oh, okay. "Well, I understand why."

Then it took 1500 sandbags to shore that levee up, but again, had I not had that *relationship with the Congressman*, and with Pete who's a personal friend, to pick up that phone and make that decision, there were 15,000 houses at risk of being totally flooded had it not happened.

Having, you know, an interesting part but, it just shows you again what Crisis Leadership has to be in tune for.

#3 - WHAT DO YOU KNOW NOW THAT YOU WISH YOU KNEW THEN?

I think that every situation is different, and every situation is a learning experience.

And I think in every situation that I dealt with, whether it was in hurricanes, whether it was flooding, whether it was a disaster, whatever it was, I think *each of those situations was a learning event.*

And I think it was a learning event for the staff because we're in that emergency operation center, well, doing Ike and doing Harvey both, we were there 24 hours a day for 10 to 12 days at a time, and sleeping, eating, and doing all those things.

And you have a working relationship with your staff that they depend on you, to be the leader, to be there, and so, I guess that the thing that I learned most was that you don't know all the answers.

And there's a different answer in every situation.

#4 - WHAT ADVICE WOULD YOU GIVE SOMEONE WHO WANTS TO IMPROVE THEIR CRISIS LEADERSHIP?

I think the most important thing that I can tell people is you need to *listen to others that have been there, done that, and have the experience that you might not have.*

Don't think that you have to do it by yourself.

It's something that you have to *depend on others who have been through it to help you do it.*

As I said before, a lot of these elected officials, especially that have term limits; they're turning over quite often. They may have never been through a crisis in their four years or their eight years, even two years. There are two-year terms for Mayors and Council. They may have never even experienced that.

My advice to them is you need to *rely on those that have been there.*

Don't be afraid to pick up the phone. Don't be embarrassed to say, "I don't know the answer to this. You have been there, and you help me."

I think the biggest mistake that elected officials make is that they think they know it all. They don't.

As I said, I spent 39 years, and every single day was a different learning experience for me, and I told people that I don't know all the answers.

I know a lot of them, but I don't know them all, and I'm not afraid to pick up the phone and call. I was very fortunate that I had some very good city managers in my tenure as mayor and councilperson. Guys who had been through a crisis before. Guys who had been through situations that I could sit down with and say, "what do you think we need to do?" I'm making that decision by myself.

Again, I go back to say, for those people that want advice, don't make those decisions by yourself unless you're sure they're right.

Because if you make it by yourself and they're wrong, you're gonna pay the consequences for it. Take some people with you. *If it's a wrong decision, say, we made that decision, not I made that decision.*

I think my best advice to those that haven't improved that are trying to improve their leadership skills is to depend on those that have been there.

#5 - WHO IS A CRISIS LEADER THAT INFLUENCED YOUR CAREER?

I think the last question is, do you have people that have influenced you over the years in making that decision?

And I have to go back to what I said earlier.

I've been fortunate to have city managers that I could sit down with and depend on to run things by.

And I won't single out one of them, because I think they all had a different thing to offer me.

My experience with all of them has been different, but I don't think there's one particular person that's had a major influence on me other than maybe my parents, upbringing, to make the right decisions for people.

KEY TAKEAWAYS:

o Accept the responsibility to make the tough decisions

o Depend on those that have been there

o Build relationships and rely on your alliances

o Know the boundaries of your legal rights

o Relentlessly serve the people you are responsible for

o Every disaster is a learning event

o One person does not know all of the answers ... ask for help

o Don't make decisions by yourself unless you know you're right

o Surround yourself with good and capable people

AMY SHICK - MILITARY SPOUSE ENTREPRENEUR

Home	Fayetteville, North Carolina
Then	Military Spouse Entrepreneur
Now	Military Spouse Entrepreneur
Contact	**LinkedIn:** amy-shick-a15a9359/
Quote	*"People First ..."*

WHY AMY IS A CRISIS LEADER

When I first contacted Amy about being interviewed, she selflessly made the case that her husband, a 20+ year US Army Infantry Officer with combat experience, would be a better fit.

While I hope to include her husband Jason in this project at some point, too, I'm sure glad she agreed to participate. The insights, experience, and competence she's gained as a military spouse and entrepreneur easily rival that of any other leader I interviewed for this project.

If you have any military experience, then you know the incredible crisis leadership role that the spouse performs, for their family, and for their extended military family. And the higher the rank of the service member, the more significant the expectations tend to be of the spouse at home.

In our interview and in our ancillary conversations, Amy spoke extensively about different "thought leaders" that inspire her to help guide her in her professional and private journey. After spending some time visiting with her, I easily place her in the same category of inspiring thought leadership, and when you hear her insights, you'll see why.

It is an honor to be able to highlight Amy Shick and her crisis leadership insights.

#1 - WHAT IS A CRISIS LEADER?

A crisis leader is someone who relies on their education, their experience, resiliency, and faith to guide a disaster or tragedy through reconstruction or recovery.

#2 - PLEASE SHARE AN EXAMPLE WHEN YOU RELIED ON YOUR CRISIS LEADERSHIP?

I actually have two examples, and I'd like to share them because they are very different from one another.

The first example happened a couple of months ago.

I live in North Carolina, my husband's active-duty Army, and he is currently deployed to Afghanistan.

We have a rental property in Tampa, and our tenants moved in. A week later, they welcomed their third baby into the world, and a little over a week after that, our tenant, with good intentions, tried to fix, or at least check out a leaky faucet.

Well, it was in the master bathroom on the master bathroom tub, and the faucet, as he started to dismantle it, exploded, and flooded the house with about 500 gallons of water. So since water takes the path of least resistance, water was flowing, pouring, raining out of every recessed light and vent hole there was downstairs.

It was a mess.

The bathroom was flooded, the bedroom was partially flooded, and the downstairs entry, living room, and dining room were flooded.

So I had to rely on my crisis leadership skills significantly for that event because, one, my tenants were involved, and they had just moved into the house, his wife was recovering from giving birth, and now we have a disaster, a destruction of property.

So that was one example of relying on my *crisis leadership skills, and that took communication, it took evaluation, it took project management, financial management,* and there were some situations that I had not dealt with before that I really had to rely on other experiences to apply to this one.

A second and very different crisis that we recently had was, in the Army, we are very far away from all of our families, so our fellow soldiers and their families become very important to us and a big part of our lives, like family.

And there's a family that we are very close with, and her husband was deployed with my husband. And they had seven kids, and their 13-year-old son had made the decision to end his life.

And it has been a very different crisis.

This is a tragedy that is emotional and psychological, and it has *required a different set of resiliency skills*, one that relied a lot on faith to get us through this particular situation.

So it has definitely been a different crisis that required different skills and a different set of faith that I've really had to rely on to get myself through it, and to guide my children through it, and be supportive of our friends.

#3 - WHAT DO YOU KNOW NOW THAT YOU WISH YOU KNEW THEN?

As a military spouse of 25 years, with several moves and many deployments, I have developed a lot of resiliency skills, and different crises require different resiliency skills.

And something that I've learned throughout the years when I'm confronted with a crisis, whether it be a destruction of property, a natural disaster versus a personal tragedy that affects the heart in humans that we care so much about, it requires two different sets of resiliency skills and leadership to guide through that particular crisis.

It really depends on what the crisis is.

What I have learned is to *step back and try to remove myself from the situation*, trying to examine what I want the outcome to look like and how I'm going to achieve that outcome, setting emotions aside, what tasks need to get done and what feelings and emotions do I need to take into consideration. Not only of my own but for the people that I am guiding through the disasters, through the tragedy. But then also who I am working with, through the disaster and through the tragedy.

So there is a difference there.

Something else I have also learned is, I journal.

I journal at the beginning, during, and even after, when there is a crisis. And that is so I can go back and I can re-visit and reflect on the feelings that I had at the moment cause it's always different going back when you are no longer in that crisis situation and what that does is it helps build your resiliency and your skillset and your abilities to handle the next crisis or situation that arises with a more well-rounded view.

#4 - WHAT ADVICE WOULD YOU GIVE SOMEONE WHO WANTS TO IMPROVE THEIR CRISIS LEADERSHIP?

What advice would you give to a leader who wants to improve their crisis leadership skills and ability?

The advice that I would give is it's just like anything. *You have to practice, you have to educate yourself, and you have to look towards other people who are influencers in this space and reflect.*

Also, build your own personal resiliency.

And that's something that, in the Army, as a military spouse, they train us. We go to Care Team training, FRG (Family Readiness Group) Leader Training. We learn a lot about ourselves, and we learn a lot about the crises.

You practice, right? And you evaluate, and you go through scenarios so that when a crisis does arise, this isn't the first time that you're looking at it.

So something that I find very helpful is I like to read different books on leadership and different aspects of leadership because there's a lot of leaders that have a lot of different leadership styles and thought leaders.

So for instance, Brené Brown, she is a very famous author, she's a social worker, and she has two books that I've read. She's got many more books, but the books that I have read is one called "Daring Greatly," and that is about your own personal vulnerability, and it's also about shame, which is a very interesting topic, and I think you'll find it very surprising how much you learn about yourself in that book.

The second is called "Dare To Lead," and that is a book about leading through vulnerability, and leaning into the discomfort, and knowing the discomfort is temporary. But by leaning in and communicating in a wholehearted and vulnerable way, you will be a lot more effective, not only for yourself but for the people you are leading.

Another thought leader that I love to read his books, and builds my own resiliency and crisis leadership, is Malcolm

Gladwell. He is famous for taking studies, social dilemmas, and tragedies, and weaving them together to change thoughts and perspectives on different things that happen in our lives every day, and we don't link them together, and we don't put them together to create new thoughts and new perspectives, which is really great.

The other thing that I like to do that I really feel builds your own resiliency and will make you a better leader, or anyone a better leader is getting to know yourself very well, your strengths, your weaknesses, your personality styles, your leadership styles.

So some tools that I've used for that is the *Myers-Briggs* personality test, the *Enneagram*, and then also the *Clifton Strength Finders*.

And what those do is they allow you to really take a look at yourself, and how to develop your own personal leadership style so that you can be the most effective and efficient leader that you can be to the people that you are serving.

Because leadership is serving those that are contributing, whether it be a volunteer or paid employees, those people are all working toward the common mission of either the reconstruction or recovery of a crisis event.

#5 - WHO IS A CRISIS LEADER THAT INFLUENCED YOUR CAREER?

Who is a crisis leader that has influenced my career?

I actually have several people who have influenced my career, what I consider on the micro and macro level.

Again, those authors that I read books, those thought leaders that I follow.

They have definitely influenced the way I see the world, the way I approach things, the way I approach situations.

My overall philosophy of dealing with working through a crisis is; people first. I feel that if I put people first, everything else will fall into place. Tasks, well, that's easy to formulate a list of tasks, but to actually take care of the people who are working through the event with you, through the reconstruction or recovery, or those affected by the reconstruction and recovery.

And also how it is affecting you personally and emotionally. I've two other sets of people on the micro-level that have really influenced me, and the first is my parents.

I grew up in a home with two emergency room nurses as parents, so they lived in daily crises. In the ER, a very busy ER with a lot of trauma.

So, hearing about their stories, hearing about how they also handled things, and how they sprang into action but how they also connected with the families of those patients. It's not just taking care of patients. You also have family members that you sometimes are delivering really bad news to.

The other thing is they also in their mid-40s started an ambulance company. And they were transporting critically ill patients.

So to see my parents, in leadership roles other than being parents, was really great for me to see that, and I learned a lot.

Not only from them but also from the employees that they were serving as leaders for their company and also the patients that they were continuing to serve.

The ultimate micro-level influencer has been my husband. He is an active-duty infantry soldier, has been for almost 20 years now. And I see the way he reacts and the way he leads his soldiers through events that are sometimes minimal and sometimes very tragic.

And, you know, as a military family, a lot of my time is spent volunteering and serving the families of the unit he leads. So we have a very intimate relationship with those families. And to see his perspective and how he leads through small and large crises and tragedies is very opposite of how I do things.

And so it's great to see how he approaches things because I learn from him. And because I've been involved in many of these situations, it really allows me to see him in a different light than I would otherwise see him as a husband or a father.

KEY TAKEAWAYS

- Rely on faith
- Set emotions aside
- Spring into action
- Remove yourself from the problem
- Educate yourself
- People first
- Define the outcome you want to achieve
- Seek out other thought leaders to learn from
- Build personal resiliency

- Lead through vulnerability
- Different crises require different resiliency skills
- Journal before, during and after a crisis to enable reflection
- Each crisis teaches us lessons for the next crisis
- Train for, practice and evaluate the potential crisis
- Assess and embrace your strengths, weaknesses and leadership styles
- Leadership means serving others

BARRY DOMINGOS -

MASSACHUSETTS STATE POLICE

Home	Boston, Massachusetts
Then	Massachusetts State Police
Now	President and CEO of All-Hazards Incident Command Solutions
Contact	**LinkedIn:** barry-domingos-5922b336/
Quote	*"Do more than the right thing, also do things the right way ..."*

WHY BARRY IS A CRISIS LEADER

Barry and I met while working on some of the same projects. His subtle but authoritative grasp of the incident command system (ICS) is unrivaled. As a result, I've frequently beaten a path to his door when I needed the most accurate and thorough understanding of ICS principles.

And I'm not alone. There's high-demand for his instruction and consultation.

The quote that I attribute to him is perfectly suited, too. As you'll see, Barry learned the importance of doing things the right way as a young leader, and to this day, he still personifies that attitude.

#1 - WHAT IS A CRISIS LEADER?

So one of the first questions is, 'what is a crisis leader?'

And I think it's a multi-faceted question.

Maybe it depends on what type of crisis you're talkin' about if we're talkin' about incident management,

I think that person has to be well educated, well-schooled, have the ability to think on their feet, work quickly, work with others, and have that leadership quality that is either trained or just deeply ingrained in that person.

The second side of that is my experience then tells me that if you're dealing with people in crisis, meaning a personal crisis, well, that takes a certain amount of empathy and compassion.

The people that would have that empathy and compassion are probably those folks that have been in a similar situation or a life situation to cause them to create that understanding, and generally, those people will make a better-informed decision that's supportive of that person in crisis.

#2 - PLEASE SHARE AN EXAMPLE WHEN YOU RELIED ON YOUR CRISIS LEADERSHIP?

So, an example of when I might have relied upon some crisis leadership.

Several examples of dealing with the public.

When I was working homicide, dealing with people that have, my last three homicides were children under the age of two that had been raped and murdered.

And in that case there, of course, you want to solve the crime, but one of the most important things is reaching a conclusion for the family that's gonna be supportive of them in the long term, and in the long run.

And sometimes that's hard to translate.

So I think that as far as dealing with that, that became, to me, a yardstick by which I would measure the success of whether or not I had done a thorough investigation, or completed that investigation properly was: *Had I satisfied that requirement, that I had done as much as I could for that family, in order to reach a positive conclusion for them* that was gonna last them for quite some time?

Because the last memories they had of their child were the most important ones. And we certainly didn't want to drop the ball and leave them kind of in a bad spot.

So, I think that kinda highlights the most important part.

The other part of that would be, some of the personnel I had working for me.

We had folks that ran through some hardship in their lives and had difficulty. We really had to take that into consideration when we're dealing with folks; if we don't, we're kinda leaving them a little bit short, I think.

#3 - WHAT DO YOU KNOW NOW THAT YOU WISH YOU KNEW THEN?

So a question comes up, what would I do now if I had, that you wish you what I knew then, and I think one of the things that I've learned over time is I've had to teach myself *to listen better.*

We tend to be in law enforcement crisis-driven, meaning you present me with a problem, I'm gonna give you a solution and probably in very short order, and I'm gonna solve that problem fairly quickly for you and for the folks around us.

We learn to do that. One of the problems with that is we don't become very good listeners.

And we really need to get to the point where you start to listen, not just in your personal life but when you expand beyond just being a responder, so to speak, and get to the point where you need to be that leader all the time.

You have to *take the time to be deliberate, slow down, listen to people, listen to their issue, their problem, the crisis that they see it, how they're presenting it, whatever their paradigm is, and their approach.*

I think it allows you to then create a circumstance where those people are going to be more effective and do their jobs more effectively because you can't do their job for them.

You have to allow them to do their job, so I think one of the things I wish I had learned earlier was just to become a better listener.

#4 - WHAT ADVICE WOULD YOU GIVE SOMEONE WHO WANTS TO IMPROVE THEIR CRISIS LEADERSHIP?

Okay, what advice would you give someone who wants to improve their crisis leadership skills?

I think, no matter what your position is in life, and I've learned this over time, *sometimes the person that you might think is the least probable to become the strongest leader in the room, a lot of times that person is indeed the best leader in crisis or otherwise.*

Some people have the innate ability to be leaders; other people learn that ability. West Point, Annapolis, we have a lot of places where we can send people to learn to be leaders, but those folks that have that innate ability, boy we really got to seek them out and develop those folks.

So, I think that what people need to do is maybe begin to look at those leaders around them, emulate those behaviors, they're gonna be positive in the long run. *The listening skills, the ability to be empathetic, exercise some compassion for other folks.*

I think those qualities make you a stronger leader, and I think from a business standpoint, nine times out of 10, if you treat your employees well, they're gonna treat your business well.

And, the same thing happens in public service. If you treat your employees well, they're probably gonna treat their service well.

Now, by treating your employees well, sometimes that means that we have to discipline them. Sometimes that means we have to take 'em aside and say, hey, not for nothing, could we have done this better? Or, did you think of this approach instead?

So, treating 'em well doesn't mean we ignore bad behavior. Sometimes it means we have to take corrective action. *It's the manner in which you take that corrective action that'll determine whether these people are gonna continue to work for you and whether you're gonna be successful as a leader.*

#5 - WHO IS A CRISIS LEADER THAT INFLUENCED YOUR CAREER?

Who was the crisis leader that influenced your career the most?

And, I remember, there was a lieutenant, an older fellow, he's still around, he still does a lot of work for our agency, but he was a very, very, very tenacious and thorough investigator.

And I remember one time, I had, someone called into internal affairs and made a complaint against me. And, it was just those types of things, where I shouldn't have gotten a speeding ticket, or, he was a little bit rude, or whatever, and, the lieutenant that came down was okay, but I asked for this other lieutenant in internal affairs, who I knew was probably the most thorough, tenacious, get-the-job-done, and probably most likely, to either convict you, or exonerate you.

And knowing that I was in a position where I hadn't done anything that really needed to be disciplined, I pushed to get this particular lieutenant.

And then years later, he became a fairly good mentor to me. And, the reason for that was because, sometimes people say, let's do the right thing. And his position was always, let's do things the right way. And I think there's a significant difference between that.

He never had the position of doing an investigation, and say, let's do the right thing, he always just said, *let's do things the right way.* And having done things the right way, I think you develop an opportunity, or a likelihood, that you're probably gonna have better success, not just in life, but in your career, by doing things just plain the right way.

KEY TAKEAWAYS

- Leaders also maintain empathy and compassion
- Be thorough; people are counting on you
- Do things the right way
- Never underestimate the leadership ability of others
- Treat your employees well; they're going to treat your business well
- How you discipline someone can determine how much of a leader they will be in the future
- Be deliberate and listen intently

Barry Domingos

Bob Martucelli - Massachusetts State Police

Home	Somerset, Massachusetts
Then	Massachusetts State Police
Now	Consultant/Instructor
Contact	**LinkedIn:** bob-martucelli-44a0309/
Quote	*"Trust your people to do what you've trained them to do ..."*

WHY BOB IS A CRISIS LEADER

"Marty" and I first met while working as a part of an instructional cadre teaching incident management to public sector responders.

He immediately impressed me - and everyone else - with his deep understanding of crisis leadership coupled with his ability to effectively communicate that knowledge.

Notably, Marty was also one of the original movers and shakers behind the Massachusetts State Police creation of a formal Incident Management Team (IMT). Bringing such monumental change to an East Coast law enforcement agency of their size provides a glimpse into the caliber of leader Marty is.

Having seen him in action both professionally and personally, it is evident how consistently he "walks the talk" as a leader of others.

#1 - WHAT IS A CRISIS LEADER?

You know what?

For me, the definition of a crisis leader is an individual who, even in the most chaotic, very confusing situations, has the abilities, has the skills to kinda just step back and just slow it down and see through it and still be able to collect the information that's needed to be successful and direct others through that situation for whatever it is, and in my career, I've noticed that some people have a natural ability to do that.

There may be another sector where people actually learn how to do that, but for me, it's that person who stares in the middle of that chaos, and for some reason, for whatever, others are directed to him or to her, and they seem to be able to take emotion out of the decision.

They *see clearly what the objectives are to be successful,* and they're able to, in a very deliberate manner, convey that information to others that they need to be successful, no matter what the situation is, and of course, as far as crisis leadership goes, Mike, that's the situation I'm referring to is something that's very demanding on people's abilities and their demeanor and their emotions and whatnot, somebody who can lead you through something like that, also somebody who understands the meaning of communication, and when I say that, these people, when I say communication, what I really mean is a really good listener, and even though they may have some authority over you, they're not afraid to just stand there and intake some information from somebody who might have a different perspective, and they understand that taking that perspective really is, the objective is just to make sure that you're making the right decision for the greater good, and you have that way with all.

We don't care who it is.

You're gonna make it your purpose to take in new information from others, so it's that being a good listener and applying that information, somebody who has some sort of command presence, and I don't mean by being some sort of a military-type like demeanor, but somebody who just has a presence about them in the way they speak, the way they dress, and especially, this person usually understands their policy and procedure, and people know that about that person, so the way they communicate, the way they hold themselves in an arena like that, a very chaotic situation.

They seem to have if you want to use this term, command presence, or whatever for lack of a better term.

They have that, but mostly, *it's being able to just stand there, sit back, make decisions, take the emotion out of it, and of course, always putting their folks first,* obviously talking about safety and all that good stuff that we know about, Mike, and that whole package.

So really, it's *somebody who can remain calm and give direction and understand that people need that direction.*

#2 - PLEASE SHARE AN EXAMPLE WHEN YOU RELIED ON YOUR CRISIS LEADERSHIP?

During my last ten years on the State Police, I was a member of our Type 3 Incident Management Team.

In the last two years, I was the team leader.

And I remember a particular case where there was a lost elderly gentleman. And he was about 76 years old. And he had Alzheimer's, but it really hadn't gripped him at this point in his life where he was, you know, he could still go out and enjoy his life. And he walked constantly. He was a walker.

And everybody in this small town knew him. It was about ten years ago.

And... one day, his mom, I mean, correction, he lived with his daughter and his son-in-law. And he would make a habit of going out and walked every day while they went to work. And he would usually be home when they got home from work.

And then one day, he didn't come home.

So, obviously, they waited for him to come home. He didn't come home. And that alerted the next steps.

They called the police and reported the situation. And then the police did that initial hasty search and talked to the family about possibly where he might go, and places he visited and whatnot.

And long story short, this went on for five days.

He was not the healthiest guy, and again, Alzheimer's was setting in, but they still trusted his ability to go out and socialize.

So anyway, there's a personal piece to this that had developed as well, because the fire chief of this community, it was his father-in-law. So the fire chief, it's his father-in-law who's missing.

And the other piece to it is, my daughter's best friend, it was her grandfather.

So there I am sitting at home watching this unfold on the news every night because Holbrook had not reached out to the State Police for any assistance at this time.

So, my daughter would call me, and she said, "Dad, what are we gonna do "about Dina's grandfather? "Aren't you gonna help?" And I said, as soon as they call us, we'll go out and help.

She goes, "You gotta find this guy. "He's a great guy."

I said, okay.

So I had that pressure on me, you know, to, you know, do something for them.

So, eventually, after five days went by, and it was in the month of April, so, you know, the temperature was okay, but it was cold at night.

So they finally called the Mass State Police Incident Management Team.

And so, the next morning, I went and I met with the family and did the usual intake that we usually do. And, what I did notice, was at this point in the search, after five days went by, if you can imagine, the family was very emotional.

And they had done all the right things up to this point. They had put posters out.

By this point, the media was involved, media stories were going out regionally lookin' for the guy.

Posters were everywhere, and they were gettin' some sightings, that he was at this restaurant at this time, and he went to that restaurant at that time at night.

By the way, he left his home; this was at night now when they realized he was missing, it was like 8 p.m. when they started the initial search on day one.

So anyway, as this went on, they finally called us, and I can remember how emotional the family was, and how emotional the father-in-law, I mean the son-in-law was who happened to be the fire chief who was involved in the search.

At that time, in those days, you know, the fire department, the police department, whoever else they called to assist in looking for them, weren't that organized, they didn't have many resources or the correct resources.

They really didn't have a plan on how to systematically look for this gentleman. And they really ran outta options.

So, with that kind of urgency, and with that kind of emotion that was being pressured on us, we set off to find, I'll call him Jack. So, as a result, and you know this better than anybody, Mike, our initial actions were to stick with the plan.

We had a plan, we had a formula for a 76-year-old Alzheimer's patient who was not in good health, with a cane, where he might be as far as a radius, as a perimeter, and we would start there. And that's what was the plan was.

But what happened was, they were gettin' these sightings from, believe it or not, a truck driver called in and said he saw him in a truck stop in Connecticut. And so, the family wanted us to go to Connecticut.

They wanted us to investigate all of these unsubstantiated locations where people were seeing him.

But we stuck with it. We stuck with the plan, and then we got the appropriate resources there, and we used our process, we didn't deviate from the process, even though we had all this pressure on us to do other things.

And lo and behold, we found him in 6.5 hours. And he was 1.6 miles away from his house. And our radius was two miles, as you know. So based on our two-mile radius, we started two miles and worked in towards the house, and we found him.

Not the other folks, you know, their intentions were right on point, obviously, but we brought that process and that methodology to it.

And the other thing we did was, we included them. We included the fire chief, the police chief, and some of their command staff into the process. Which kinda gave us some validation that we knew what we were doin', and they validated that they knew we knew what we were doin'.

So I guess as far as the leadership goes, we had the wherewithal to understand what they were going through, and to understand that this was a very emotional event for them. But for us, it was something that we were used to, and we knew that we had to stick with that process, and also satisfy their emotions with our compassions, and sitting down with them, and involving them.

And that's how we always did that kind of thing. And it held true.

You know, so the leadership part, as I said, was just stickin' with the process, takin' the emotion out of the equation, stepping back, writing our objectives, and staying true to our methodology, even though we were gettin' all these pressures to do it a different way.

And we were very successful in doin' it that way.

So, you know, we always second guess ourselves when we're out there trying to do something like that, and it doesn't go right, and you say, maybe I shoulda done it a different way, or maybe I shouldn't have done it that way.

But this was, again, nine times out of ten, if we stuck with our process, and stuck with, you know, that leadership from Incident Management Team perspective, for folks who really didn't understand this process, it just validated it to us that this was the appropriate way to make this stuff work.

So that was one incident for me, Mike, that I could probably define as a crisis leadership moment, you know, for us as a team.

And other small stuff, again, but other things similar to that.

But that was a big lesson for me to learn, *to stay true to your training, and not exclude the people you're tryin' to help*, but involve them in a way where they feel like you're satisfying their concerns at the same time.

On the other side of the coin, *you're sticking with your methodology and your training,* so.

#3 - WHAT DO YOU KNOW NOW THAT YOU WISH YOU KNEW THEN?

Like all of us, not just me specifically, not like me specifically, but I think all of us, when we're new to our jobs, especially public safety jobs, police, fire, EMS, when we first start that job, in our early years, everything we do, everything I did, had that sense of urgency to it that I had to complete it, right now, and, you know, take action, right now.

And that's how we used to do it as young guys on the jobs.

As you may know, and now that I think about it, back then, even then, I think, *I wish I had the presence of mind at times to just slow down and stop and think rather than act initially.*

I think that would've helped in some of my situations where I was successful, but I probably could have done better with more information, made better decisions.

So I think it's hard for young folks to really understand the fact that most times, *99% of the time, you have time just to stop, process the situation, and take in new information.*

Use that information for your decision making, and then take action. So I probably could have done that better, or used that better, when I first started as a police officer.

So yeah. Also, *understanding the fact that your decisions have an impact on others as well.*

So, if I had made a better decision, if I made an arrest, well that arrest is going to affect a lot of other things, and it may affect other people in the barracks, as far as what they had to do with the arrest, the arrestee's families, et cetera, et cetera.

They're all appropriate, but I probably could have done it better if I just stopped, thought about it, and took in some new information and acted on that.

So I wish I had known that then, that nothing has to be done right away, unless it's a life-threatening situation, of course, I'm not talking about that.

Take the time to think about your next actions.

I wish I knew that then.

#4 - WHAT ADVICE WOULD YOU GIVE SOMEONE WHO WANTS TO IMPROVE THEIR CRISIS LEADERSHIP?

Some advice.

I think, looking back at my own experience with folks that were my supervisors at the time.

I think I was always drawn to the folks, or I *trusted the folks, who really knew their job*. They really knew their policy and procedure to be quite frank. If you know there's somebody that knows the job inside and out and know their policy and procedure, that somehow gets transmitted throughout the ranks. 'That guy or that girl, they really know what they're doing.'

So I think, for me, *learn your policy and procedure* and know it because the people that you're working with, if you're in that crisis leadership position will believe in your decision making 'cause they'll say 'That guy knows what he's doing.' or 'That girl knows what she's doing.'

So I was always attracted to that person, that knew their policy and procedure.

As a result of that, I was a real book guy.

Because of that, I always wanted to know what my policy and procedure was.

Because I had faith, you know, in my early years, in that person, whoever that person was at the time.

The other thing I would advise them is if there is somebody in your world, especially on your job, who has those qualities that we were talking about earlier, about that crisis leadership qualities, take what you like, and emulate it into your own response, or your own way of doing things.

You know, use that to improve your crisis leadership if you notice something else in somebody else.

I remember as a young guy in the military or coming on the job, there were some instructors in my life who, uh, I- I used their methodology in some of the things that I did later on in life because they were so successful in what they did, I said 'Yeah, that's the way to do that.'

And so I used it.

What else?

I think if leadership, you know if you're interested in leadership, there's nothing wrong with studying leadership.

There are all sorts of ways to understand what a good leader is.

There's a new term out there these days. Well, it's an old term. I know you know it, Mike.

Being a servant leader and having a servant's heart as a leader and understanding what that really means, I think, is good advice for somebody who- who wants to or- wants to or has to lead others in a crisis.

If you understand what that means, you'd be much better off, and people will believe in you.

So that servant leadership attitude, I think, is good advice for somebody to understand what that means.

You know, another thing it probably was being on the state police, there's a lot of little things that you do that matter to others.

So the way that you present yourself on and off the job will build your credibility with others.

The way you present yourself, the way you wear your uniform, whatever uniform that is, that all means something to people who are looking for direction. And if you're very consistent with that, on and off the job, in the building, or out in the field being called on in some sort of situation, it all comes together at that point where those little things matter to people that you're leading.

And you'll have established credibility all the time with these people by the way you handle yourself professionally and off the job, so all of that matters.

So that's some advice I would give to these folks.

#5 - WHO IS A CRISIS LEADER THAT INFLUENCED YOUR CAREER?

So a crisis leader that influenced my career.

There were a couple actually, but one that comes to mind was, at the time, I was in tactical operations.

I was on the motorcycle unit and we were very fortunate on our agency to have a very built-out tactical operations, which included an air wing, a mounted unit, a dive team, a motorcycle unit, et cetera, et cetera and we had this young Major come in and take over tactical operations and what I remember about him was exactly some of the things I was just talking about as far as some advice on if you were gonna be a crisis leader.

What I meant was when he came in, all of the things I just mentioned, he wore his black BDUs wherever he went, but the way he presented himself to us and his demeanor I guess is the point I'm trying to get, his demeanor was professional but yet personable because you knew that he was going to make some changes on how we did things, but you knew that the way he did it was going to benefit yourself personally.

So each member would be, I don't care if you are on the motorcycle unit or the canines or the Marine unit, his message to us was for us to be more proficient in what we did and that he was going to make sure that we were all successful, and the way he communicated that to us was completely different than the previous commander of tactical operations, and he just instilled that confidence in us in that we were very well-trained and that you could tell that in any situation.

If he were there on the scene, you would be automatically drawn to wait for his direction because he knew what our capabilities were.

He knew we were very well-trained, and the way he would deploy us and use us was a very methodical process way in where he did things, and actually, he introduced the Incident Command System to us in 1995 was [inaudible] motorcycles.

So his name was Jim Ross, and I'll never forget him.

I'll never forget the way that his leadership skills, including that servants' leadership, were much different from an organization like ours if you can imagine. That servant leadership was not even thought of in some of the old school ways of leading in the field, you know.

It was my way of the highway, and this guy brought in a whole brand new approach to leadership in the field, and he was one of the guys that I took clues from as far as leadership skills and how to handle yourself in a crisis situation.

He was the major tactical operations.

KEY TAKEAWAYS

o   Handle yourself professionally on and off the job.
o   Be consistent and available to maintain credibility with those that you serve.
o   Maintain a servant leadership attitude.
o   Take the time to think about your next actions.

o Stick with the process and stay true to your methodology.

o Remain calm and understand what is needed.

o Learn from other leaders, including the military.

o Slow down and think.

o Start well to finish well.

o Trust your people to do their job.

David Brownell - Iraq Canine Program Manager

Home	Aubrey, Texas
Then	Iraq Country Canine Program Manager
Now	Kennel Master
Contact	**LinkedIn:** david-brownell-627a269
Quote	*"It's through failure that you're gonna learn."*

WHY DAVID IS A CRISIS LEADER

I can easily make the case that meeting David 25 years ago set me on a path of successes that I still enjoy to this day.

When I started exploring Search & Rescue (SAR) teams back in the 1990s, I had the opportunity to join a team that would let me attend searches with my dog right away. I also had the opportunity to join a team that would require me to first train under the strict guidance of an authentic, widely-respected, no-nonsense, task-master named David Brownell.

I chose the latter, obviously. What I learned from David formed the foundation of what has become, for me, an unbelievable and humbling career in response, emergency management, and crisis leadership.

David has traveled on a diverse journey, as well. In our interview, he highlights a couple of examples of his leadership, but his humility - and some OPSEC (operational security) - puts some of his other leadership experience left unsaid.

From his official bio:

> "... Senior Canine Trainer and Canine Program Manager
> ... 35-year background in search and detector dog team

handling, safety, training, and management; he has organized canine programs for police departments, volunteer SAR groups, and corporate security ... knowledgeable in a wide array of canine detection fields to include narcotics, explosives, IEDs, patrol, human remains, SAR/Disaster, and missing/lost persons ... has worked over 13 years as a canine program manager and senior trainer for international security in Iraq and the Middle East ... organized and trained hundreds of personnel and detector canines and assisted in staffing and managing numerous canine projects to include the US Embassy in Baghdad, the Baghdad International Airport, and several commercial oil exploration projects in Iraq and Kurdistan...."

Besides our interview, one needs only to ask others that have ever met or worked with or for David about their experiences with him. His reputation as an authentic, no-nonsense, taskmaster remains highly respected after all these years.

David's consistent role in doing the right thing at the right time for the right reasons makes him the best kind of crisis leader.

And his lessons continue to create a legacy for those of us to follow.

#1 - WHAT IS A CRISIS LEADER?

Okay, what is a crisis leader? I think that's a good question.

I think it can be a lot of different things.

I think a *crisis leader is somebody that has both the knowledge and the skills, the ability, and the willingness to take action when there's some type of crisis.*

A crisis can be something big, it can be a natural disaster, it can be a mass shooting, it can be a local search that you don't know, or it can be somethin' that you can be crisis leader as a member of your family.

The North Texas area, we get a lot of tornadoes and severe weather, and it might be where you're the leader of the family, and you're taking to action to keep your family safe, or it can be something in your job, but you have the willingness and the knowledge and the ability to take the appropriate action when needed.

It can be a big incident, or it can be a small incident, but I think you take action when action is needed, and you have the training, either formal or informally, to know what to do, and you take it at the proper time.

#2 - PLEASE SHARE AN EXAMPLE WHEN YOU RELIED ON YOUR CRISIS LEADERSHIP?

An example where I relied on my crisis leadership, a couple comes to mind.

Early on in my career - I joined the military in 1981 - I became a military police officer.

I had just gotten out of basic training, and I was assigned to my first duty station. My partner and I were doing an evening time routine patrol of one of the military housing areas, and we had just entered the housing area.

We were coming driving through the housing area and we noticed that two vehicles were kind of driving erratic and pulled off the side of the street and one of the vehicles pulled alongside the other and fired a gunshot into the driver's window and we were probably, maybe 40, 50 yards from this when it happened.

We witnessed it.

So we didn't know at the time what was going on.

We heard the loud gunshot.

We didn't know it was a gunshot at the time. So the suspect vehicle ended up speeding away.

So we approached the driver that had been shot, and my partner went around to the passenger's side. I went around to the driver's side and noticed that the driver had been shot through the left front shoulder and so I immediately applied a pressure dressing, and we called for backup to seal off the housing area.

We called in backup.

They said there was only one way in and one way out of the housing area. So we sealed off the housing area, waited for backup and waited for the ambulance and once the backup had arrived and the ambulance had arrived and had taken over treatment of the wounded soldier, I was able to get a complete description of the vehicle and a license plate and once the backup units arrived, we started going door to door through the housing area looking for the suspect vehicle.

After about a two hour search, my partner and I noticed a garage door to one of the housing units that was only shut about halfway, so we looked inside the garage, and we noticed that the vehicle matching the suspect's vehicle description was in the garage, so we backed off, called in for backup.

They surrounded the house and sealed off the house, and they were able to make the arrest of the suspect.

So I think that's part of... That kinda started my career in emergency management and response. And it's just *applying what I had learned in basic training at the time.*

And it just goes back to, when something happens whatever you do, your reactions have to be secondary.

You can't really think about it.

You have to be able to react and know what to do and when to do it. And so that's one incident that comes to mind.

Another incident was in 2003, in February of 2003, I was with the Texas Task Force 1 FEMA USAR team, working a FEMA dog, and I was also part of a local search and rescue team, Search One Rescue in the Dallas area.

In February 2003, the shuttle crashed and broke apart over North Texas, and so we were called, the Texas Task Force 1 along with multiple teams throughout the state of Texas and nationally, probably thousands of responders were asked to go to West, or excuse me, to East Texas to look for the shuttle that had broken apart.

But also, more importantly, they were looking for the remains of the astronaut.

We deployed to East Texas for ten days as part of the task force, and I was tasked as part of a response, we call it the Black Hawk Brigade, to East Texas.

It was three or four of the dogs that were tasked to look for the remains. And basically what we did, is we were tasked to Black Hawks, and we'd go up in the air, and the FBI and the local aviation assets would go up and mark with GPS where they saw buzzards circling and so we'd deploy in the Black Hawks.

We set down the GPS coordinates with the dogs, and we'd fan out in probably about a half a mile to a one-mile radius with the HRD dogs looking for the remains of the astronauts but also looking for parts of the shuttle because there were certain things that they were interested in recovering beside the astronauts. And so I was tasked to a small team of three or four dogs over these ten days and some of my team members.

This was their first basic really massive type search and so I think the crisis leadership was just helping fellow team members that hadn't really experienced this kinda search and what to do and what not to do and basically how to handle the day to day search, not only from a tactical operations aspect but also just on a daily basis.

And I remember our task force leader was retired military and so one of the things that he was stickle on is clean uniforms. And I joked with my team members about... We were working 12 or 14 hour days, and I remember talking to my team member when we got to the hotel.

We were tired, we were wet, we were muddy.

And I remember telling him, I said, okay, the first thing we're gonna do before we go to bed is we're gonna get our uniform ready for the next day, make sure we've got a clean uniform and we're gonna polish our boots.

We were way knee-deep in mud every day and as dumb as it seemed is that appearance because this was a nationally televised event.

That professional image and appearance were critical.

So every day when we showed up to search besides knowing what tactically and operationally to do, that professional image of wearing a clean uniform with shined boots because that image is important, not only to the media and to our task force but to how other people see you and view you as a professional.

If you come in looking like a dirtbag and you're wearing the same uniform every day, even though you're dirt tired, at the end of the day, you don't get a second chance to make that first impression.

And so I think that's just the very minute, but it's the little things, I often think that makes the biggest impression. Not necessarily the big actions that you do.

So I think just imparting the importance of that, and it goes back to my military training. That's what was ingrained upon me in the military is that image, and it's... *If you don't pay attention to the little details, you're not gonna pay attention to the big details.*

#3 - WHAT DO YOU KNOW NOW THAT YOU WISH YOU KNEW THEN?

What do I wish I know now that you wish you knew then?

[sighs] I think a lot of things.

I think one of the big things, the takeaways that I've learned over the years. I spent the last three years, 13 years working in Iraq as a civilian contractor, as both a handler or a trainer or project and program manager. I think it all ties in together from what I learned from going through basic training as a private through my almost 19 years with a local search and rescue team.

Started in the K9 program, and then going on to civilian contracting.

It all ties in together for emergency management.

The lessons that you learn from the very smallest search to the largest search are the same. But I think the key thing is never quite learning. You've always got to continue learning in your education, no longer how long you've been in it. Or even if you go into a different aspect of emergency management.

With the lessons that I learned as part of the Texas Task Force One, and in with Search One Rescue, I applied, when I first started working in Iraq, I first started working in Iraq in October 2003, and a lot of just the preparation things that I learned from the task force, you know, check your gear, or make sure it's serviceable.

Same thing in the military, you know, the saying "One is none." So make sure you've got redundant systems.

I applied that with what I did in Iraq.

Always making sure you're accountable for your people. Make sure you know where your people are.

I applied those lessons, you know, when I was with the task force, when we were on searches, but also on when I was with the local search team, we were on searches.

And I apply it 'til this day.

In Iraq, you know, I can remember some of the searches that I went on, when I first started work in Iraq, some of the Knock and Cordon searches that I went on, making sure my gear was ready, making sure I had backup comms, make sure I had backup radios, make sure I had redundant first aid kits, make sure everybody on the mission knew what they were doing, and where they were going. What's the rally point if you run into problems?

So I think it's realizing that everything you do in your emergency management service career, whether you're first starting it, or whether you've been here for 40 years, is you're continuing learning those lessons.

But always continue learning, and don't ever forget the lessons you learned 30-40 years ago. Always continue learning and striving to be better.

And make yourself, not only better but your team better, because if one member of the team fails, your team can fail. You're only as strong as your weakest link.

You've gotta have everybody on the team. And I think one of the things that the task force system in the military is good at, is teaching the newest member should be able to step into the position above him, and be able to fulfill those capabilities. So, cause if you've only got one person that you're relying upon, what happens if that person is taken out of service, or can't make the mission, you've gotta have people that can, that are capable, but also willing to step up and fulfill that position.

So you gotta have redundant personnel systems, too. And to rely on it.

But I think it goes back to is never stop learning. You've always got to be continually improving yourself and don't rely on what you did yesterday because technology changes, and it improves our response capability.

Technology's a great tool, but one caution I would give as an example is everybody's reliance upon GPS nowadays, well, don't forget your map and compass. That's the core skills. Don't rely upon your cellphone GPS, cause what happens if that goes down, or if you're in an area where you don't have a cellphone signal. Or what happens if you're in deep east Texas woods, and you don't have GPS signal? Pull out old school, don't forget old school with a map and compass.

You know, old school is there for a reason. And don't become too reliant upon technology to solve all your problems.

You gotta go through old school ways sometimes.

#4 - WHAT ADVICE WOULD YOU GIVE SOMEONE WHO WANTS TO IMPROVE THEIR CRISIS LEADERSHIP?

What advice would I give someone who wants to improve their crisis leadership?

I think it goes back to education and skills training, continually strive and improve your own experience and education and training.

And also too, is don't be afraid to reach out and network with other experienced people. I think, in any discipline, you need a mentor. Find a strong mentor to take you under their wings and give you guidance.

Reach out to as many people as you can.

I remember when I first got into search and rescue, I would attend a lot of national canine seminars and for the purpose of furthering my education but also networking, and I met a lot of great, experienced people over the years.

You share ideas, techniques, and methods because what works for us in Texas may not necessarily work for somebody in Colorado, but there's something that they can do. Or even though I don't do avalanche training here in Texas, there's probably techniques and training that they're doing in avalanche training that I can apply and alter and adapt.

So I think *continually network and improve your skills* and education and just don't be afraid to fail.

I think sometimes, especially in the canine's world, we get afraid to go out there and fail.

But to me, if you're not failing, if you're always going out and you're setting up training where you're not pushing your own boundaries, you're not learning.

It's through failure that you're gonna learn.

If you're always succeeding, you're not necessarily learning a lot, and you're not expanding your comfort zone. You gotta get out there and expand your comfort zone, and I think some of the best lessons that I've learned over the years is through my failures. And it's through the failures that I've learned to become better.

But don't be afraid to fail, and there's nothing wrong with failure.

The only thing wrong with failure is if you let it keep you from trying to improve or if it keeps you from going out there and challenging yourself because you're afraid to look foolish in other people.

Most everybody that's been in any emergency management response capability has had failures, and it's *through our failures that I think that we learn some of our greatest lessons.*

So don't be afraid to fail.

#5 - WHO IS A CRISIS LEADER THAT INFLUENCED YOUR CAREER?

Who is a crisis leader that influenced my career? I can think of two people coming into mind.

One of the first ones is my friend, and I call him my personal mentor, Dr. Mark Marsolais.

I met Mark Marsolais when he was a sergeant with the Houston Police K9, and he was in charge of their patrol division K9, and he came up to the Dallas area, and we met through some friends of mine and Mark's we had in common, and Mark wanted to expand the patrol capabilities of their K9s to human remains, and so my friend Kevin Henry put Mark in touch with me, and Mark was an experienced police officer K9 SWAT sergeant and had a lot of experience.

But he really I think influenced my career because, number one is he had some of the strongest ethics and morals of anybody that I've been experienced with, and I think your ethics and your morals and your standards are extremely important in these industries, especially in the K9 field.

There's a lot of people that do unethical things or things that really shouldn't be going on in the field, especially in the field of K9, and he influenced me just by leading by example.

It goes back to the *military adage that you lead by example*, and he always leads by example, and he wasn't afraid, even though he was a sergeant with a lot of experience to come up to expand his knowledge base, and the sergeant that came with him was an experienced police K9 trainer with probably 30 years of experience, but they both came up with the desire to learn a new area.

And especially, I was a civilian, I was in police K9, and they weren't afraid to sit down with somebody that was a police K9 trainer and listen to what they had to say.

So he had, and still does to this day, have a strong influence on my career and what I've done, both as a friend, but also as a mentor, and he's led by example.

And the other I would say was Mike McKenna.

I met Mike when I was with the local search and rescue team. He was a green dog and a young pup, I would say, and I continually challenged Mike.

And when I first met Mike, I would basically, I was kind of standoffish, and I would make him show me that he was serious about learning, and he was, and he proved himself.

And he's gone on to probably do more with an HRD (Human Remains Detection) dog than I have ever done in my career.

He's had more finds than I ever did, and I take a lot of pride in that, and as an instructor, I always want my students, and I think an instructor and a teacher, we want our students to go on and be better, and to do more than we've ever done, and he has done that, and he continues to do that today, so I take a lot of pride in the fact that I had a small part in his career development.

I watched him over the past 20 years as a friend go on to mentor other people, and what I call 'pay it forward,' and I think in our industry, this is critical, paying it forward.

I spent time showing him and teaching what I know, and he's gone on to carry that forward with what he does today, with not only doing it at a task force level, but he's done it in his professional life, and I take a lot of pride in doing that.

KEY TAKEAWAYS

- Find a strong mentor
- Sometimes you have to do things 'old school'
- Create and rely on redundant systems
- Never stop learning
- Continually network and improve your skills
- Pat attention to the little things
- Lead by example
- Don't rely on technology to solve every problem
- Pay it forward

Greg West - Assistant Chief; LA City Fire Dept.

Home	Newberry Park, CA
Then	Assistant Chief; LA City Fire Department
Now	Adjunct Instructor
Quote	*"Never stop learning ..."*

WHY GREG IS A CRISIS LEADER

I've worked alongside Greg teaching some courses, and his classroom presence is admirable. Almost every student leans forward on their elbows, waiting for the next nugget to be shared. When you read his interview, you'll see why.

Greg has always made time to lend an ear, offer feedback, or be of service. And always with focus, attention, and a smile on his face. Greg is the consummate leader and the boss we all wish we had at least once in our career.

Greg's stories will have you on the edge of your chair. You'll feel almost every emotion hearing his experiences as a crisis leader. And you'll see why so many people have such unabated respect for Greg West.

You'll also hear the reverence he has for the leaders that he looks up to, a true testament to the 'paying it forward' theme that is part of his character.

I had the opportunity to drive with Greg through some of his former response districts in Los Angeles not long ago. It was clear that he left a positive legacy in that fire department and city, and it's an honor to include him in this interview project.

#1 - WHAT IS A CRISIS LEADER?

Crisis leader. That crisis being, there's a lot at stake.

In my profession in the fire service, lives are at stake; property is at stake.

The wellbeing of the people who work with and for me is at stake, and the leader part has really given me pause, because when I started thinking about all this, it was, I just fell into the focus, and maybe the trap, of they do what I tell them because of who I am, that I outrank them, that I, they all work for me, that I am designated as whatever it might be, unified commander, section chief, branch director, whatever, and I kinda got away from that, because, like many of us, I've seen high-ranking officials that aren't really leaders.

And, as I thought it over, I thought a leader is somebody who can drive people to do what they want them to do, because of several factors of technical competence, first of all.

Their ability to communicate with, collaborate with, listen to, and deal with people, and I think that listening is a big part.

You have to be a good listener, too, to understand your people and know how to communicate with them and convince them that they can follow you, and you're looking out for them, and they will be safe.

I think part of that, being a leader, is decisiveness, courage, and the ability, and the wherewithal to make good decisions, and even change some of those decisions based on information or intelligence that comes in, or input from somebody who's working with or for you.

So, and that takes some courage sometimes to say, this is what I had in mind. This is the way I usually do it, but based on what you're telling me, I'm gonna make a change.

And, I think part of that leadership is, you have to *be good at what you do, that's that technical competence thing, but you have to demonstrate it.*

You have to be out in front. You can't lead from behind.

So, that leader is somebody who's demonstrating through training, through education, through practice, that the leader understands what it is that needs to be done, because they can do it too, and they've got the courage and confidence to stand in front of coworkers and subordinates and show them that I've got this, that I can do it.

Part of that leadership is *being systematic*, and working as a battalion commander in Hollywood, the systematic part came back with really, really good results several times, because everybody knew of the five companies responding to a reported fire incident, they knew where I would put the first and second engines, where first truck company would go, the second truck company.

And, what made me feel really good about it is responding to incidents from a long distance, and as I heard the assignments being made by the company officers prior to my arrival, it was working just the way I would've done it if I were there, and it was kind of a validation of my system and their trust in my system, and working with what we had in place, and we all worked on through the years, over five years I worked in Hollywood.

And I think the last thing is *never to stop learning.* I will attend the same classes as a lot of my subordinates, and I'll be in there with them.

You know, good example is I have a picture of me that I look at all the time, a high angle rescue class that I attended with urban search and rescue folks from Los Angeles City, and the first time anybody went over the cliff, well about a 60-foot drop, in a lowering operation with a rescue Stokes basket on my lap.

I was the only guy there in a white helmet, or a command officer's helmet, and I was the first one they put over the side, and that meant a lot to all of them, and it sure meant a lot to me.

So, that's a long way around to talk about a crisis leader, which is so much different than just being a command officer.

#2 - PLEASE SHARE AN EXAMPLE WHEN YOU RELIED ON YOUR CRISIS LEADERSHIP?

I'm starting as a paramedic and leaving as an assistant fire chief.

I've looked through my memories, through my slide tray, as it were, of things that happened and it's easy to go to the emergency incidents, but there are so many different times that I really had to stand by my beliefs and do what I had been trained on, and what I knew was right.

And demonstrate that I was that crisis leader, and I've got different examples of different scenarios.

Chronologically speaking, back in 2000, I worked for over a year on the Democratic National Convention Planning Group in the City of Los Angeles for the convention coming to town, and I was the second in command of the Fire Department contingent, and we were there with law enforcement, and Department of Traffic, and EMS, and people from the state.

And I hope he never sees this, but my boss and I had very different leadership styles.

For pretty much everybody in the office, about 60 people in the office, they found it very hard to work with my boss, communication-wise, and the ability to compromise on things, and I became what was known as the buffer. And I had to stand up, and we agreed to disagree on a lot of things.

And the funny thing was that this chief had been a staff chief for a long time, took Fridays off. And we worked all week because we had so much to do. So, the team became my team on Friday, and we came to call it Hawaiian Shirt Friday, looking out for the troops because nobody in any other discipline wore a uniform except the fire department people.

We were trying to stay under the radar. Friday was my day, and it was Hawaiian Shirt Friday, and we would work all day long, and toward the end of the day, we would go next door to a fish restaurant called McCormick & Schmick.

And every Friday, I bought the first round. *So, it was a $100 bill every single Friday and worth every penny of it because the team knew that I had their back, and we were gonna get this done, so, and everybody else in the office saw it, too.*

That's one.

The most emotional one is me as a battalion chief working in the San Fernando Valley, where I grew up in Northwest Los Angeles.

And in making the rounds on a Saturday and visiting fire stations, we respond to 1,400 dispatches a day in the City of Los Angeles.

And they're coming and going all the time.

I heard one for a drowning, and I recognized the street because it was about four blocks from where I went to high school, and it was about six blocks from where we were.

So, in the middle of the day in December, we heard a drowning dispatch go out, and we were the closest, and I knew it.

And it's funny, or it's not that we all promote to get out from under all of those EMS runs and go to the exciting stuff, but this is a drowning.

I'm six blocks away, I'm miles closer than the two resources, and I added Battalion 17 to that incident.

And my staff assistant, the driver, questioned me on it. What are we doing?

And I just said we're doing the right thing. Let's go.

And we found it on the map, and we got there to where a three-year-old had drowned in the hot tub in December in very, very cold water.

And as I controlled the parents who were absolutely distraught and trying to interrupt the CPR we were trying to do. My partner performed CPR on this three-year-old, who, after we put her in the ambulance after the paramedic engine and the paramedic ambulance arrived, she's breathing on her own, and she went home nine days later.

What brought it really close to home is on Valentine's Day a year and a half ago, they brought some cardiac arrest survivors and their rescuers to the fire department on

Valentine's Day, and I got to meet little Tracy, who was a high school senior at the time.

And it was one of the most rewarding. It wasn't a big fire, but if we *put life safety as our number one tactical priority*, we nailed it.

And we did it.

I went out on a limb, and I did things that everybody, I'm sure, out on the radio said what's the chief doing going out to a drowning?

And it was the right thing with the right outcome, so very emotional for me.

Then going in chronological order, I responded to Hurricane Katrina with California Task Force 1, 70-person, an urban Search and Rescue team sponsored by FEMA.

And we mobilized in six hours, went out the door, were escorted by the Highway Patrol all the way to the California border to get there as quickly as we could, and ended up in Dallas, yeah, in Dallas, where they put us up in a hotel with three other Urban Search and Rescue Task Forces for two-

and-a-half days because FEMA logistically wasn't convinced that they could support us.

And they made the decision, right or wrong, it doesn't matter, they made the decision to hold us off until we could go in and not be more of a problem, but be part of the solution.

And 69 people on the taskforce just did not understand that, and they weren't happy with staying in the hotel and waiting around, and not being able to do what they were trying to do, and they drove over 2,000 miles for.

And the *crisis leadership part was letting them know that we were doing everything we could to get to work, letting them know exactly what was going on and why, and taking the abuse, and the unhappiness for it.*

And the toughest part for me is at 2,000 miles away with me responsible for all of them, and I couldn't afford for anybody to get hurt. We all had to get there safely and at 100% capacity when we finally were deployed. And we were in the Mississippi Gulf Coast.

I wouldn't let 'em use the gym; I wouldn't let 'em play basketball. If they wanted to exercise, they could do pushups and sit-ups, and they could walk the stairs, but I couldn't have a sprained ankle. I couldn't have a muscle pull, and they did not like me for it, but they all understood.

And that's that courage part of being a leader, and I've got a last one.

I know this is a long answer, but what's important to me is that shortly before I retired, I responded to a fire in a grocery store late at night, about 11:30 at night.

And as I was going to the store, I thought of the Phoenix Fire Department, where they had lost a firefighter in a grocery store.

And I was commenting to my staff assistant about these never have a good outcome.

And sure enough, we had an attic fire in a fairly large grocery store. The lights were still on. They were still getting the shoppers out of the store when we got there.

And we kept looking at the fire coming through the roof with the truck companies up there ventilating the roof, which made it look even worse.

The lights are still on, we can see the firefighters inside working, and at the point where the lights went out, I was depending on a lot of conversation and reports from inside, which we didn't get.

And ultimately, when I saw the smoke coming out the front doors, which were 10 feet high, I ordered everybody out.

And all but one came out, and he was on the radio calling for help and screaming, and on the edge of panic, but that firefighter was doing everything right.

His company went back in, and they rescued him. Within 30 seconds of getting that firefighter out the door, the building flashed over, and it came really close.

What we got out of it was the chance to interview a firefighter who should have died, and we had just a mere miss.

My boss responded with, what's the big deal? You got 'em out.

And my philosophy is when you make a mistake, stand up to it and tell everybody what happened, so they don't make the same mistake.

There are a million mistakes to make out there for any first responder, Fire Law, EMS, whatever it might be, military, don't make that mistake.

And we pulled all the tapes together and all of the diagrams together and shared it with every officer in the fire department. So, I had to stand up there for months with a training battalion chief and a training captain. And that training captain actually took it to the Firefighters Union to get some support for us to put this program on.

And we taught the lessons of the Vallarta fire on accountability and communication to every officer in the fire department.

Those are my four where I truly had, I call it rowing my own boat, but I did what I had to do.

#3 - WHAT DO YOU KNOW NOW THAT YOU WISH YOU KNEW THEN?

Things I wish I knew then that I know now.

And the one that came to mind that, a quote I heard after putting on the presentation for the Vallarta near-miss fire was that *the higher you go in rank, the more of a coward you should become.*

And it was so profound to me and so obvious, and I was almost ashamed that I didn't ever define it like that, but, my position was to put people in harm's way, to put them at risk, and I did take it very seriously, and I very much cared about my coworkers, my subordinates, members of both, all the first responders.

But that short quote so clearly defines the incredible responsibility as a first responder in a command position, and, it, I wish I knew it then, as I was responding to that fire, what I was gambling with. Because I'm on the outside and I'm gambling with dozens of firefighters on top of and inside that burning building.

#4 - WHAT ADVICE WOULD YOU GIVE SOMEONE WHO WANTS TO IMPROVE THEIR CRISIS LEADERSHIP?

Improving your crisis leadership is so multifaceted.

You have to be good at what you do.

You have to demonstrate that you assess the level of risk, you assess what needs to be done, and you can clearly communicate and collaborate on how we are going to get that done.

You can't be a leader if you don't have people to follow you and understand that they want to do what you know needs to be done.

So, and they won't do it if you're not good at it. And not only being good at it but being out front.

That I said before, you can't lead from behind, so when we are working through dangerous operations, be out there with them.

Don't assign the training and walk away.

Be confident and give them confidence.

I think if you want to improve your crisis leadership, learn to be a good listener because a lot of people have different perspectives and ways to get things done, and they work. So you can listen and actively learn.

I had a chance to see James Comey put on a presentation in my hometown, and he said one of his keys to success was his ability to listen actively, to engage the President of the United States when he was listening, not appropriately, and not be afraid to ask the tough questions to clarify what was going on.

So I think being a good listener to those who work around you, and by actively listening, you're working on communication, you're working on that collaboration of we are in this together.

And as your leader, I'm gonna make sure we get through this because I care about you, and I'm gonna look out for you. I'm gonna make sure you know your job and can do it, and we'll do it together.

#5 - WHO IS A CRISIS LEADER THAT INFLUENCED YOUR CAREER?

I've had the chance to work and learn from some great leaders in the fire service, especially in Los Angeles.

The first name that came to mind was, well, he retired as an assistant chief, Jim O'Neill.

I worked with him when I was a young, very immature, you know, be described as wet-behind-the-ears captain. And initially, just watched and just listened, and he did the same thing.

He just watched me, and he listened to me and gave me time to prove myself to him. And he was a great teacher, a great mentor.

And what I learned from him is when somebody is striving to, not to please you but to be like you and to learn from you and not let you down, he was very demonstrative in his letting you know that you, kid, you're doin' all right, you know?

And to see the chief come out of his office at Fire Station 27 and walk out and put his arm around me and say, let's take a walk, kid, here's what you do.

And I knew I had it made at that point. I knew it was going to be okay.

And a lot of growin' up took place in the two years that I had the chance to work with Chief O'Neill.

I'm going to add two more to the list.

A fellow instructor at TEEX, at Texas A&M, named John Nowell. And John and I worked together from the mid-'70s until we retired in 2008 to 2010. And we worked together. He worked for me in the last few years in the fire department and absolutely a leader of men and women.

That he *doesn't have a plan for every single situation that could ever come up, but he works from a process of looking out for the good of the men and the women who work for him*, be it on a strike team out of the city or within his battalion.

He truly cared, he truly took care of them, and sometimes, at the expense or even spiting some of the leadership because he had a clear standard of what he knew was right and wrong, and looking out for people who worked around him was a big part of that.

And he *had the whole package, the technical competence, the ability to communicate, the ability to know his feelings through body language. He didn't even have to open his mouth, and you knew his position.* And everybody else did.

And the last but certainly not least is a retired captain from the fire department named Jim Featherstone.

And I jokingly say that I outranked Jim Featherstone for my entire career, and I worked for that man my entire career. He was a leader within the firefighters' union. He was a firefighter or a leader within the emergency management community, within the training community.

And he, there was never any doubt that he had everybody's best interest in mind at keeping them well-trained, at keeping them safe, at looking out for them, even representing them in the disciplinary process when he felt they had been wronged. And sacrificed so much of his own time to look out for the other members of the department, to go outside.

99

He used to bring into captain's meetings military programs that we could apply to my battalion and to the fire department of how they handled logistics, how they handled communications.

He was always out there looking for new and better ways to get things done. And I'm a better person, and the department is a better position for all of the efforts that Jim made.

He was rewarded by a position as the City of Los Angeles Emergency Manager. He served an interim position as the fire chief, just unprecedented to retire as a captain and later be appointed as the interim fire chief.

And he was very effective and well-liked within the department. And now, he's in the private sector pioneering GIS and a lot of computer-related approaches to how we can do better as first responders.

KEY TAKEAWAYS

- Great leaders are also great listeners
- Be ready to change direction when better information is available
- Lead from the front
- Be technically competent at your job

- Build repeatable systems to increase operational efficiency
- Never stop learning
- Be creative when engaging your subordinates
- Do the right thing, always
- Listen actively
- Analyze your mistakes and share the results to reduce a recurrence
- Be out in front, not behind
- Make life safety the #1 tactical priority
- The higher you go in rank, the more of a coward you should become
- Be systematic
- Demonstrate confidence, and your subordinates will feel confident
- Always look for new and better ways to get things done

HARRY LaROSILIERE - MAYOR OF PLANO, TX

Home	Plano, Texas
Then	Mayor of Plano, Texas
Now	Mayor of Plano, Texas
Contact	**Facebook:** PlanoMayorHarry
Quote	*"Crisis leadership requires real-time decision-making ..."*

WHY HARRY IS A CRISIS LEADER

I met Harry and his soon-to-be wife Tracy in 1994 while volunteering for the same service agency in Dallas. It was clear from my first contact with Harry that he was an authentic man of service and leadership.

Harry's authenticity is the first thing people notice about him. And his achievements illustrate his endless capacity for service.

Even though the demands on his time are extraordinary, when you're speaking to him, he makes you feel like you are the only person in the room.

You'll hear Harry mention the importance of our inner compass for us to navigate with Integrity, Intelligence, and Intent. From him, it's not just advice; it's also how he lives his life. Very, very authentic. In a crisis, this is even more evident.

As the twice-elected leader of one of the nation's largest cities, Harry radiates leadership competence. And his insights into what makes a leader successful are one of many attributes that separate Harry from other elected officials and further cements his legacy as a leader among leaders.

#1 - WHAT IS A CRISIS LEADER?

A crisis leader is a person *who takes action at the very moment that action needs to be taken.*

A crisis leader is someone who may not actually know what needs to be done but knows that something needs to happen, and they take the initiative and accept the responsibility.

#2 - PLEASE SHARE AN EXAMPLE WHEN YOU RELIED ON YOUR CRISIS LEADERSHIP?

An example of a crisis leadership moment for me was back in 2017 when we had a council member who put a very racist and Islamophobic post on Facebook.

And I knew at that moment something needed to be done to show value to all our citizens. Not only the Muslims in our community but everybody.

I found out early that morning about it. I attempted to reach him, and he did not respond to my calls. And I called a press conference at 1:00 and asked for his immediate resignation.

And it was important to do that in a very swift and decisive way because the *ramifications of inaction were far worse* than if my call for his resignation was right or not.

The reality is crisis leadership when you're in that moment is real-time decisions.

Sometimes *when you're making a critical decision, it may not actually be the best one.*

And others around you, your *team may not understand all the variables that are in play.*

But as a leader, it's up to you to assess it, filter them, and then decide what's the best thing to do or not to do.

Very often, though, *rarely is inaction the best decision.*

#3 - WHAT DO YOU KNOW NOW THAT YOU WISH YOU KNEW THEN?

What I know now that I wish I knew then is that *leadership calls for you to be prepared all the time.*

There's no manual to prepare you for the unexpected. And so the *reliance on your confidence and abilities in yourself is the ultimate manual you have.*

There's an inner compass in you that tells you whether you're operating out of integrity, intelligence, and intent.

And as long as those three are met, then you will always get to the right place.

#4 - WHAT ADVICE WOULD YOU GIVE SOMEONE WHO WANTS TO IMPROVE THEIR CRISIS LEADERSHIP?

The advice I'd give to someone who wants to improve their crisis leadership skills is the same advice I'd give to just anyone looking to improve pure leadership skills.

And I call it the Four L's of leadership. Leaders **Listen**, Leaders **Learn**, Leaders **Lead by Example**, and Leaders **Let Go**.

So in order for you to be an effective leader, you have *to listen to your team.* You have to get their input; you have to get their feedback. You will ultimately make the decision, but in order to get their buy in to complete the task, you have to listen.

Leaders learn by virtue of taking action. You learn from your mistakes, and you correct your course.

Leaders lead by example. You have to be the first one in, last one out. You have to work harder than anyone.

The example I always say if there's a pile of rocks in one corner that you need to take to the other corner, you just start picking up the rocks. You try to pick up the largest one, and all of a sudden, people will all of a sudden want to help you and assist you. And the last one, which is the hardest one, is leaders let go.

And what I mean by that is in order to be a truly effective leader, you have to let go of the process.

And leaders by nature tend to be controlling. But if you micromanage, you will not empower your team. But if you listen, learn and live by example, then it's incumbent on you to *step away and allow your team to execute on the plan.*

And I say four L's.

The fifth one I say jokingly is the fifth L is after you've done all those things, the best leaders leave.

Because *a true leader, what they do is they don't build followers, they build other leaders. They cultivate other leaders.*

#5 - WHO IS A CRISIS LEADER THAT INFLUENCED YOUR CAREER?

Two crisis leaders influence me and my life.

I am a big proponent of having mentors, and if you don't have a direct mentor, I believe in virtual mentors, and so one of them was Dr. Martin Luther King.

He operated in constant crisis.

Sometimes he created the crisis to lead through it, and he had a plan, and he had a resolve to see it through in a manner that most of us probably could not do.

And the other leader, someone who I was fortunate to meet, is Colin Powell.

He and I have so many similarities in our background. We both were born in the West Indies, both grew up in Harlem, both studied geology at City College in New York, and then our careers took different paths. I became mayor, and he became, I think, a five-star general and Secretary of State.

But he faced a lot of different challenges and crises, and he also was very process-orientated.

He operated with integrity and intelligence, intellect, intent, and all the things that you need to be grounded before you make decisions.

So those are the two people I look at towards emulating their leadership skills.

KEY TAKEAWAYS

- Operate with integrity, intelligence, and intent
- Take the initiative and accept the responsibility
- Benefit from direct and virtual mentors
- Inaction is far worse than being right or not
- Build leaders, not followers
- Rely on your confidence and abilities when something unexpected occurs
- Crisis leadership requires real-time decision-making
- Leadership calls for you to be prepared all the time
- Four L's of Leadership: Learn, Listen, Lead by Example, Let Go

Jeff Armentrout - Vice Wing Cmdr; US Air Force

Home	Charlotte, North Carolina
Then	C-5 Instructor / Aircraft Commander
Now	Vice Wing Commander; 302nd Airlift Wing; US Air Force (ret)
Contact	**LinkedIn:** jeff-armentrout-9b869811/
Quote	*"Training makes missions successful ..."*

WHY JEFF IS A CRISIS LEADER

Jeff's leadership roles have spanned the majority of his life. Really.

As an Eagle Scout, he served as a leader of other boy scouts both during meetings and during friction-filled campouts and long hikes.

As a cadet in the Air Force Academy, he served as a leader among his classmates and spent his off time leading treks up and down the Rocky Mountains on multiple day hikes and mountaineering trips.

As a mountaineer, he led himself and others to (and from) the highest peak in North America (Mount McKinley) and returned with nary a scratch.

As an officer in the Air Force, Jeff has flown and commanded missions critical to our nation's defense.

As an expert in aircraft ergonomics, he led improvement efforts to make the piloting some of the world's most complex machines a little bit more user-friendly.

As an international commercial pilot, Jeff routinely makes leadership decisions that instantly impact the 100's of passengers in his charge.

Did I learn this from my short interview with Jeff? No. I've known Jeff Armentrout since junior high (we also earned our Eagle Scout rank on the same day). Not only is he one of my oldest friends, but he is one of the first people I wanted to speak to when I first started this interview project.

Read on, and you'll see why.

#1 - WHAT IS A CRISIS LEADER?

So, to me, a crisis leader is someone who is prepared to deal with the crisis for which he's trained, or he or she is trained.

It's someone who people look up to typically I would say *they are the calm in the storm* if you will.

In my profession, both military and civil aviation, all of us are highly trained so that when we are faced with a crisis, we are able to react appropriately without panic setting in or derailing us from taking the correct actions to deal with the crisis that we're facing.

In terms of team leadership, I think a crisis leader has to instill trust in his team and, more importantly, has to empower the team.

In the current leadership team that I'm a part of, we use the three words *empower, trust, and accountable, or to shorten that E.T.A.*

So, we empower the team, we trust the team to do the right thing and to do the thing that they're trained to do, and then we hold them accountable for their actions.

And I think that's a critical piece of crisis leadership is empowering the team, trusting them to do the right thing, and then holding them accountable at the end of the day.

Something that I think is really critical for crisis leaders is the ability to *remove barriers for others*. And I think that applies to any leadership role, but that is one of the things that the team really needs the leader to do is to tackle those obstacles that are standing in their way of getting their job done, and the leader is responsible for trying to remove those barriers.

A crisis leader that is at the top of his or her game is going to practice his craft as often as he or she can, and will *always seek to improve*, and you see that in what we do in the military where we're continuously practicing and exercising and always trying to get better.

And also in aviation, *we're always training, we're always trying to improve our skillset, and always refreshing our skillset so that we're not ever caught off guard* or by surprise when we're faced with a particular crisis.

#2 - PLEASE SHARE AN EXAMPLE WHEN YOU RELIED ON YOUR CRISIS LEADERSHIP?

1 of 2

So as an aircraft commander in the Air Force, I was flying the C-5 Galaxy, which is a large cargo airplane.

And we were flying a mission from the East Coast of the US over to Europe. Crossing the Atlantic, roughly about halfway across the Atlantic, we had a strong smell of fumes from the back of the airplane.

So one of my loadmasters, and a loadmaster is someone who's responsible for both the passengers and the load on the airplane, we carry three loadmasters and a total crew of about ten people plus we had probably about 70 passengers on the airplane plus all the cargo.

But loadmasters went down into the cargo compartment to investigate the source of the fumes, and they found that there was a fluid leak coming from one of our cargo pallets, and it was leaking fluid all over the floor, so.

The smell of fumes was very strong, and it was starting to overwhelm the loadmasters, so at that point, as the aircraft commander, I started looking at options as to where we could go with the airplane. Our best option at that point would've been to divert into the Azores, which was probably a couple of hours away.

And so, the upfront crew started looking at what those options would look like.

And the loadmasters went to work; they donned their portable oxygen bottles. And they started dealing with the leak in the back. They were able to break apart one of the cargo pallets, and they discovered in the middle of the pallet, several containers of paint thinner that were leaking all over the cargo compartment.

So at that point, I directed them to do the best they could to clean up the leak. And the flight engineer was directed to start performing the smoke and fume elimination checklist. Which basically ventilates the airplane and helps get the fumes out of the airplane.

The loadmasters were able to isolate all the leaking containers and put them in some garbage bags to isolate the leak and then they were able to, get the rest of the fluid that leaked on the cargo compartment cleaned up with some pads and some rags to get all that off the floor. Fumes dissipated and, we talked as a crew about what we wanted to do, the loadmasters felt that they had sufficiently isolated the leak.

And, we made the decision to continue on to destination and had no further issues with the cargo at that time.

In terms of the crisis response, what made it successful was really, the training that the crew had received throughout our career.

And me as a crisis leader, letting them do their job and trusting them to do their job and everybody did an outstanding job, and we train this way, all the time.

To work as a crew and to let everybody take a functional leadership role based on their expertise. It can be fairly complex 'cause it's a fairly large airplane and me as the aircraft commander, I can't see what's going on in the back, I have to rely on the loadmasters to tell me what's going on.

So communication is vitally important to help everybody get a common picture of what is going on. And once everybody has a common picture to work from, the crew is able to effectively work towards achieving the goal or the end goal that we're going for. Which in this case is, get the airplane back in a safe configuration and safely execute the mission as planned.

So I guess I chalk it up to good training, good communication, and me trusting my folks to do their job, which they all did.

And a successful outcome as a result.

2 of 2

A little less of a crisis, but some of the same principles apply.

I was a leader on a scout (Boy Scouts of America) trip. We were doing a backpacking trip in Colorado. We were climbing a 14,000-foot peak.

The plan had been to start early in the morning, summit the peak probably around ten o'clock, and then spend a couple of hours descending the peak by a different route than we actually climbed the peak.

That would get us, basically, a complete a loop, and get us back to our camp around noon, hopefully, so that we could get on with the rest of our itinerary. So, we were able to get up the peak and got to the top. I'm looking at the map, we had decided or, I guess, I had decided as the leader of the trip, that we would take what appeared to be a trail going down the backside of the mountain, that would complete the loop.

So, as we were coming off the summit, there was a faint footpath leading through a scree field. After about two or 300 feet of descent, the trail essentially disappeared, and we find ourselves in a very large scree and boulder field, with no clear path down off the mountain.

At that point, we were faced with a decision to climb back up or continue down, and we talked about it. I was convinced, at the time, that we would pick up the trail once we got off the scree field, based on the map that I had, there was a very clear trail and clear route back.

Nobody really wanted to go back up the three or 400 feet that we had already lost. Everybody was pretty tired from the climb, at that point. So, we elected to continue down.

About halfway down the scree field, it became very challenging, lots of loose scree, and rocks were coming loose and rolling down the field. I had one come within probably a foot of hitting a scout.

That boulder was moving, it was probably about a foot in diameter, and it was probably moving about 20, 30 miles an hour as it went zooming by one of my kids. Very scary, at the time, thinking that if he had been hit, it would have taken us a very long time to get any kind of emergency response back there.

We managed to get off the scree field after, probably about two hours of very slow-going. It was probably noontime. Everybody was hungry and tired. We paused once we got off the scree field, finished off what water we had, and ate some lunch, and then continued down. Tried to find a trail.

I could not find a trail, so we just did some map reading, got ourselves into a dry spring bed, and then followed the spring bed back around until we were able to intersect a trail that got us back to our destination.

Couple things about that whole incident, number one, the *preparation was key to keeping us from getting into a true crisis situation.*

We had plenty of water, we had plenty of food, and we had plenty of daylight to give us time to navigate back down that side of the mountain, and back down to where we knew our camp would be.

I think some of the other things that helped prevent that incident from getting more serious was the preparation of the boys and the adults. Everybody had prepared very well, in terms of their fitness. Everybody was very deliberate and very careful in getting down. We gave ourselves lots of time, we didn't rush and were able to keep everybody calm and not too worried about the fact that we weren't on a trail.

Cool heads prevailed, and everybody was a little bit better for having had the experience, but, nonetheless, the lesson learned was, if you're not sure the path down, go back down the way you came up.

#3 - What do you know now that you wish you knew then?

As I get a little more senior and a little more into higher levels of leadership, probably one of the biggest challenges I have is learning how to delegate things better.

And I think that's essential to crisis leadership, especially when you're leading a fairly large team. And so, I think at the point I am right now, one of my big lessons learned is that you don't have to do it all and you don't have to know it all.

And that really comes down to knowing your team and using your team and leaning on the expertise within your team, because a leader can't know everything and is certainly not a subject matter expert in everything.

So, clearly, using that functional leadership and empowering those functional leaders to do the tasks that they're the best at is one of the key things that I would suggest to anyone that's taking on leadership roles for larger teams.

And it goes back to that ETA: **empower, trust,** and **accountable** in terms of how you lead your team and how you're successful in dealing with any crisis that a team is facing.

#4 - WHAT ADVICE WOULD YOU GIVE SOMEONE WHO WANTS TO IMPROVE THEIR CRISIS LEADERSHIP?

Anybody who wants to improve their priceless leadership has to embrace continuous learning, and I think one of the most critical things is always exercising your skillset.

And the way we do it in the military is we train like we fight. So making it as realistic as possible, as close to the real thing as possible, is critical to improving your leadership skills.

So any opportunity you have, whether it is a small-scale exercise or a large-scale exercise, to put your team in the situations to challenge yourself, and don't be afraid to fail in those exercise scenarios, because that's where the learning occurs, by identifying your weak spots, both personally and amongst your team.

I think it's important to learn your resources, know your resources, know your team as best you can, and always seek to improve your knowledge and your expertise.

As I said before, don't stop learning and always seek to learn more.

#5 - WHO IS A CRISIS LEADER THAT INFLUENCED YOUR CAREER?

I've had several leaders that I thought were outstanding crisis leaders and influenced both my development and my career.

One of them I can recall is a man named Mike Cox. He was an instructor pilot that I flew with when I was a young pilot in the Air Force.

I was on a mission with him when we were in Europe and got re-tasked to do a crisis response into Africa for a developing situation where we had to evacuate US citizens from a country in Africa that was evolving into chaos if you will.

One of the things that impressed me about him and that I took away is that he *put the mission at the forefront.*

He put everybody on the team into action in terms of doing their piece of it to ensure that we got the mission off on time, that we planned the mission appropriately, and that we got the assets on the ground, which were, essentially, Special Forces with helicopters and ground vehicles, to go in and evacuate the non-combatants.

Some of the key things that he did, and it goes back to some lessons that I've learned and the things that I think are important in crisis response, is that he empowered the entire team to go off and do their things because time was critical, so everybody had to take a piece of it.

He couldn't do it all. Everybody had to do their part. He made it very clear to the team what had to be done and why it had to be done and why it had to be done in a timely manner so that we could execute the mission rapidly and effectively.

We got the mission off the ground, and we got our team into the airfield that we were going to ahead of schedule. We got them off our airplane, and we got out of there as quickly as we could. It was an impressive turnaround, and it was one of those things when you see all the pieces come together, all the piece parts, and everything works like a well-oiled machine because of our training, our expertise, and the leadership that was on the various teams that were executing at that time.

KEY TAKEAWAYS

- You don't have to know it all or do it all
- Empower your team
- Be the calm in the storm
- Train like you fight
- Don't fear failure, that's where learning occurs
- Embrace continuous learning
- Rely on checklists
- Training makes missions successful
- ETA: Empower, Trust, Accountable

- Remove barriers for others
- Practice your skillset
- Communication is vital for a common operating picture
- Trust your people to do their job
- Preparation is key to avoid a crisis
- Delegate
- Put the mission at the forefront
- Lean on the expertise within your team

Jeff Moster - Managing Dir.;

Financial Services

Home	Chicago, Illinois
Then	Vice President (Financial Services)
Now	Managing Director (Financial Services)
Quote	*"Relationships are everything ..."*

Why Jeff is a Crisis Leader

In the years that I've known him, it would be a rare day indeed for Jeff Moster to be out-hustled or indecisive about something.

His leadership qualities are evident in everything he does, whether playing sports, mastering his career, or devoting energy to his family and friends.

Jeff's crisis leadership was baked-in at an early age. For example, experiencing the unexpected loss of a parent at a young age activated Jeff's enduring resilience and personal leadership, which he has relied on throughout his life.

He personifies my favorite Russian proverb:

 "The same hammer that shatters the glass forges the steel."

As you will see, overcoming significant professional challenges also demanded more from Jeff's resilient personal leadership. At a time when others in his position simply walked away, Jeff's strong character and purpose prompted him also to lead those around him who were desperately looking for direction.

Though he would like to defy the label of crisis leader, Jeff embodies everything we look for in a leader in times of turmoil: resolve, decisiveness, and courage.

#1 - WHAT IS A CRISIS LEADER?

A crisis leader is someone that does whatever it takes, does whatever is required to facilitate as positive of an outcome as possible during times of great stress.

They are someone that's willing to put the mission in front of themselves, and they are adept at synthesizing information that can be coming at them very quickly.

Lots of different sources, lots of different variables, but they can synthesize that information quickly, and they're capable of *confidently and concisely communicating what needs to be done* as a result of taking in all those different variables and communicating that to who is affected and what needs to be done.

#2 - PLEASE SHARE AN EXAMPLE WHEN YOU RELIED ON YOUR CRISIS LEADERSHIP?

An example of a time that I was involved in some crisis where I needed to exhibit some leadership was after the infamous Lehman Brothers bankruptcy.

I had been an employee of Lehman Brothers since 1998, and I was with them until their bankruptcy in 2008. And that was an absolutely crazy time in my industry, the financial world.

I managed money for clients, and their monies were tied up at Lehman because of the bankruptcy. Because of the unique nature of that firm going bankrupt, their funds were tied up during the bankruptcy process at Lehman, and they needed help.

The problem was, I, as a former employee of the company, was forced to leave. I couldn't stay there, and so I left Lehman to go to another employer, and then that left me in a very precarious situation where I had old clients that needed my help, but contacting them would violate a non-compete I had with Lehman.

Even though Lehman was bankrupt, the bankrupt estate felt that there was a duty for me to remain at arm's length.

Having said that, no one was left at Lehman to help these old clients of mine.

They're in complete disarray, they're panicking, they don't know what to do, they don't know what's going on with their money, and aside from people's personal relationships, their family, their friends, money tends to be pretty high on people's priority, so I was dealing with something that was quite emotional with people, and I was in a very difficult catch-22 place because I had legal obligations to not talk to them, but I had what I viewed as a *moral obligation to help them.*

So, I was in a situation where I elected to take the risk of violating what was technically a legal uh, legal arrangement that I was not supposed to violate, and then went ahead, and on multiple occasions, had conversations with people, told them what I knew, helped them as much as I could, knowing that if someone on the other side, from the estate of Lehman Brothers, wanted to get nasty with me, that there probably was that possibility that could hang over my head.

But at the end of the day, *I just couldn't, in good conscience, leave them hanging in the lurch, knowing that I could help them in some manner.*

#3 - WHAT DO YOU KNOW NOW THAT YOU WISH YOU KNEW THEN?

So something I know now that I wish I knew then was the fact that even when you're in the middle of a crisis, and you're making decisions that you know are based on fundamental right versus wrong, you're doing the right things for the right reasons, you're doing the best you can, and the truth seems so clear, you have to anticipate that if there's another side to the crisis that the creators of that crisis or the people involved on the other side of the crisis ironically may in their self-serving, selfish interest turn the whole situation on its head to make you look like the bad guy in the middle of this chaos.

So even though you're doing what you know is best and that helps you proceed steadfastly with a clear conscience, be aware *that the world's not perfect and some people, in their own self-interest, will perhaps try to put the blame of the crisis back on you.*

#4 - WHAT ADVICE WOULD YOU GIVE SOMEONE WHO WANTS TO IMPROVE THEIR CRISIS LEADERSHIP?

So some advice I would give to someone that's trying to enhance their crisis leadership is to the extent that time allows document why you're doing what you're doing. Who you're talking to, why you are making the decisions you are.

Be communicative about the decision-making thought process.

As much as you can try to get decisions that you're making in writing.

Get the reasons you're making these decisions placed in writing.

If you're relying on information from other parties to be making the decisions you're making get that reliant, get that information you're relying on in writing such that you will not need to be questioned about why you're doing what you're doing down the road.

#5 - WHO IS A CRISIS LEADER THAT INFLUENCED YOUR CAREER?

I was involved in a business that was not working out, and this was years ago.

The business needed to be shut down, and the leader of this business had done a masterful job of developing relationships with not just myself, but my coworkers, other leaders across the business.

And he truly had a magnetic personality, a flair for leadership, a tremendous gift of oration, and had done a phenomenal job of getting us to believe in him. And as a result, we were very willing to trust whatever direction this individual thought we should go, for the future of the business, that would ultimately be shut down, but he was going to try.

The attempt was to try to make this business be shut down in the least complicated way possible.

And what I learned from that is that *relationships matter significantly.*

And this somewhat ties into the previous question about advice. So to the extent, you're a leader. If you have excellent relationships with those that you're involved with, your ability to lead them is gonna be much more enhanced to the extent that you're invested personally, and they trust in you.

In this case, we believed in this leader so much that we went along with his direction, and it turned out to be a situation that wasn't necessarily best for us, but he had done such a good job of navigating where the business needs to go, his objective was accomplished, and we had all gone along for the ride.

But it just shows *the importance of relationships and trust,* and how that can help leaders have followers do just that. Take it where the leader best believes they should be.

KEY TAKEAWAYS

o   Put the mission ahead of yourself

o   Decide and communicate quickly

o   Always do what's right

o   Be wary of other people's self-interest and what it may motivate them to do

o   Confidently and concisely communicate what needs to be done

o   Document the data behind your decision-making in writing

o   Build and maintain excellent relationships and trust

Jimmy Kane - Deputy Chief; FDNY

Home	New Hyde Park, Long Island
Then	Lieutenant; New York City Fire Department (FDNY)
Now	Deputy Chief; FDNY (Ret)
Contact	**mailto:** 5kanes@optonline.net
Quote	*"Take time to make time ..."*

WHY JIMMY IS A CRISIS LEADER

In his career, Jimmy Kane rose to one of the highest ranks in one of the world's largest fire departments, FDNY (Fire Department New York). And not by accident.

His insights and instincts for how to lead effectively provide an outstanding road map for anyone interested in improving their leadership acumen. As a crisis leader, his career included earning a spot as a team leader on a team of other leaders, the FDNY's Incident Management team.

Like nearly every highly capable leader I spoke with, Jimmy is personable and communicative without losing their effectiveness.

There's no doubt that the FDNY is a better department because of Jimmy being there just as there's no doubt we will all be better leaders by embracing Jimmy's lessons.

#1 - WHAT IS A CRISIS LEADER?

You know, you sent these questions, and we could all give the book answer, what is a crisis leader?

And it all depends, in my mind, it depends upon what profession you're actually from.

And mine is going to be centered around being a member of the fire department, being a member of an incident management team for a fairly long time.

Book, I guess, a quick book definition is the *ability to lead when the world around you is in disarray.*

I'd like to attack this question from a different point of view, and maybe not a different point of view, but just to list what I think is necessary, some necessary qualifications, or some necessary things that a crisis leader needs to be. And I'm going to start with a couple of categories together.

First, they have to *be calm, even-tempered and keep their emotions in check.*

Reason being behind this is your subordinates and your superiors will all react to you. If you're not calm, if you're all over the place and you don't look like you have an understanding of what's going on, they will react in the same way. If you are calm and even-tempered, they will feel that they will have more confidence in you, figuring that you have the knowledge and ability to handle what's going on. So I think those are three things that right from the start you always need in a crisis leader.

The next group I would talk about would be, you need to *be courageous, decisive, and look at the big picture.*

And by that I mean, *you are going to be making decisions under duress with incomplete information all the time, you're never gonna have all the answers.* The big thing that goes on with this one here is, some of the decisions you make are gonna be unpopular. And I guess a quick little example of that would be at a large scale fire scene where units are inside thinking they're making headway and you're making that decision to go to an outside operation. That's gonna be a very unpopular decision with those people that think they're doing a good job, but you have to have the courage and the foresight and to make that decision and stand by it.

Next, I'm going to go to *listen to others and especially listen to others that have an opposing view from you.*

People have a tendency to think that they have a full understanding of what's going on, and sort of get into almost like a tunnel vision. Even though they may not be in full tunnel vision, but if you listen to people that are looking at it from a different angle or from a different perspective even, it gives you another whole picture of what's going on. You're constantly evaluating, and you don't have, you are not afraid to change course if things aren't going well. And you're willing to take ownership of the fact that things weren't going well, so that's why we're taking a different direction here.

One thing that's really important is you never make a promise to somebody that you can't keep; *you always give honest answers.*

If you're not in complete control yet, or if you don't have a full handle on this, don't let your superiors think that you have. Tell 'em we're still trying to get a handle on this, you know we're working on it and tell 'em exactly where you are in your mind and where you are in the operation, and make sure that they understand that we're still working on it. Don't let them think that you're further along than you are.

One thing that's always very big and probably should be up at the top is always making sure you protect your people.

And probably the biggest part of that is making sure you protect them from themselves because as emergency responders, all we want to do is solve the problem. And the younger you are, the more invincible you think you are, the more chances you'll take, so I guess this question, this part of the question goes right back to risk a little to save a little, risk a lot to save a lot.

It's easier for you as the crisis leader to see those differences, so it's, that's where I'm going with protecting your people, especially from their decisions.

Next, I would talk about, *make sure you're basing all of your decisions on what's best for everyone and the organization, and not what's just best for you.* You're not what it's all about; the outcome is what it's all about. And how you get there is important, but it's always important that the outcome is what's best for everybody and not just you.

And the last thing I would have to say about the crisis leader is: *always maintain a positive attitude.*

Don't take things personally during a crisis because things aren't always gonna go your way; you're gonna get blamed for a lot of things. It wasn't your fault, but if you maintain that positive attitude, then people will understand that, that you do know what you're, they do know that you do know what you are doing.

So, that would be probably my definition of a crisis leader.

#2 - PLEASE SHARE AN EXAMPLE WHEN YOU RELIED ON YOUR CRISIS LEADERSHIP?

Okay, so I'm gonna talk about what, in my mind, is probably the first time I ever really had to rely on my own crisis leadership, and that's just going to go back way back earlier in my career, I think it was, I'm not sure the date, it was either 1991 or 1992, somewhere in that area.

The beginning of the summer, I was a fill-in lieutenant, I think I had maybe just over a year in the rank, I was still what we call a covering lieutenant in New York City, which means you fill in where is necessary.

I was actually working in 28 truck, in what they call UFO, which is "until further orders." I was filling in long-term for another lieutenant who was out on medical leave.

So, on this night, and I know it was early summer, 'cause it was extremely hot, I remember that. Night order began at six o'clock, somewhere around 6:30. We get a phone alarm for a building fire that's well past our first due area, and it's probably a box where we would be fourth-due. Meaning it would be a second alarm assignment for us, and we were going as the first-due truck.

What we didn't realize was there was already an all-hands fire that we were gonna be responding past, 'cause it hadn't been announced on our dispatch system yet, because they were just getting there as we were being notified of this box.

What was going on in the city at this point was, the day before, a drug dealer was shot by an undercover cop, and the community was saying that the usual, that the cop was at fault, and everything. My memory is very clear on this, is that the cop was cleared of everything, and he was in danger of losing his life when he shot this guy, but Washington Heights at that time, in the early '90s, was a very tough neighborhood, we'll say.

So, they lost it behind the drug dealer, and actually, Mayor Dinkins at the time stood behind the drug dealer, which complicated issues also.

But here we are, we're responding up, and we're coming into the area where we're passing the initial fire, and we go and light some sirens, and the chief on that scene says, "Turn the sirens off, turn the sirens off!" I'm on my radio, saying, "But we're responding past here." He goes, "Turn your sirens off; you don't want people knowing you're coming!"

So, I had no idea what he was talking about. So, we responded five blocks past this fire, turned into a block to get to the address we were going to, and we still had two blocks to go.

The address we were going to was actually on a dead-end street.

As we got a block away, before we got into the dead-end street, I all of a sudden realize what he was talking about. We were being attacked from people in the neighborhood, throwing stuff at the rig as we were going down the block, and actually the guys in the back of the rig at the time were like, "Oh, what's going on here," you know, it was just a little bit of like a blasé attitude with them, you know, figuring it was just some kids drumming stuff at the firetruck.

Well, when a five-gallon pail of whatever came off the roof and landed right in front of the rig, I realized immediately we were in trouble. I turned to the chauffeur and said, "Get us out of here, get us back to 'quarters."

Now, we were a good probably two miles from 'quarters, which, in this response area, is a long way, 'cause it's tight streets and everything. But the guys in the back of the rig are

going, "Where are you going, we didn't get to the box yet."
And I'm going, "I don't care, we're going home."

And they were giving me a little bit of a hard time, and all of a
sudden they saw another bucket come off the roof, and
they're going, "Oh my god!" And they realized where I was
going.

So, they understood then that the decision I made, you know,
instantly on that spot was we have to get out of here, was the
right decision.

Now, when we get back to 'quarters, my immediate boss was
working at another fire, so I had nobody to notify at that
point. And his boss was the deputy at that fire, so I would
report to a battalion chief who was at the fire, who would
report to the deputy chief, who was also at the fire. So, I have
no one to contact as an immediate supervisor, so my decision
at that time was, I made two notifications. First, I told the
dispatcher to put it over the air that there's a riot condition
going on up in Washington Heights. And the dispatcher goes,
"What are you talking about?" So I said, "I'm sure you're
gonna be getting multiple calls shortly," and they did. So they
were unaware of the situation.

And my second phone call was to Fire Department Operations Center, which is in our headquarters, and told them, "We have a severe situation going on up in Washington Heights." So, coming from a lieutenant, you know, the staff chief on duty, took it upon himself to try and get ahold of the chiefs on the scene. So, we had the dispatchers contact them, and ask one of them to call him. So, one of the chiefs, I don't know which one, got on the radio, somehow got on a phone, you know, in the area, because there were no cellphones back at the time. Or, if there were, I wasn't aware of them. [laughs]

But they got ahold of headquarters and said, "Yes, he is 100 percent correct, we have a problem going on up here, we haven't been able to get out of here to notify anybody, but yes, the notification process should start, we are in an all-out riot situation."

So, we had a procedure, you know, the fire department had a procedure, AUX 138 it was called, and it was in case we had riots and stuff in the city. It was a, we had certain quarters which were big enough where we could handle extra rigs and stuff like that, but this one became so large, we had eight task forces respond to our firehouse. Well, we were actually included in one of them.

Now, each task force included two police cars, one at the front, one at the back. A battalion chief, two engines, and one Ladder Company that would respond to alarms together. So everybody was in a line, going together. Which, you know, I think about that now and go, it just made us an easier target than coming from different directions. But it worked that night. I mean, so there were eight task forces set up. And that was, you know, the original box was 6:30, by the time I got back to 'quarters, it was probably ten to seven.

By 8:30, we were in this full emergency situation, where the chief of department and the chief of operations were actually at our 'quarters running the whole operation. And they were actually using me, I don't know what the best terminology would be, but I guess almost as a subject matter expert for the area, because I was the only one that had been out there, and seeing what was going on. And they were actually taking my advice, as to response patterns, and stuff. You know, areas we should avoid and things of that nature until they could get more and better reconnaissance out there.

So, from 8:30 to 6:30 in the morning, we had eight long teams, eight task forces, whatever you want to call them, responding on a rotating base, because as you responded, and you finished, you would come back and get back in line. My particular task force, we went on nine runs between 8:30 and 6:30 in the morning, following just in turns. So every one of those eight task forces went on, you know, eight or nine responses throughout the night. Which, if you stop and think about it, it's a very large number of responses.

And it wasn't an ordinary response, because we were in a war zone, there's no other way of saying it.

There were main blocks, Broadway, which is a main block, it's four lanes, two lanes in each direction, and a center island. We were serpentining in and out of garbage cans on fire, car fires pushed into the middle of the street, building fire, you know, we were going to building fires. We were under orders; the only thing you stopped and put out was a building fire. Or, if it was impinging on a building, you put that fire out. Otherwise, you let it burn and get outta there. Just go, make sure people weren't in danger, the building wasn't on fire, and otherwise, you came back.

Things were so bad in the streets that we had the tire mechanic there, and he replaced nine different flat tires that night, with all the stuff we were driving over just to get back to 'quarters. I remember getting a flat on one of our runs, and the first thing the chief said was, "Can you still drive the rig?"

I said, "Yeah." He goes, "Get it back to quarters; we're not stopping here." You know, so it wasn't an outside tire, it was one of our inside tires, so it wasn't that bad, but the tire was changed before it was out next time to respond, and so things were working like clockwork.

But it's a night I'll never forget, I mean, there were responses we were going on, where the gunfire, you know, there was gunshots everywhere. They weren't necessarily aimed at us, but when you're in that situation, you don't really realize that you know, you hear the gunfire, you see everything that's going on.

We've always been known, even during the bad times, when the cops were having issues, the fire department's here to help you. So, we never had those issues before. But now we're not stopping to put out the fires. We're just running by it, so nobody knows what's going to happen.

So, it was so bad that they even had police helicopters flying over, because they had so many people on the rooftops with the guns and stuff, trying to get them off the roofs and stuff.

And like I said, this was a long, long time ago, but it has stuck with me throughout my whole career, parts of it seems like it was yesterday, I'm sure I'm leaving out a lot of details, but like I said, I believe that was probably the first time I had to make decisions that I would consider as decisions made by a crisis leader.

#3 - WHAT DO YOU KNOW NOW THAT YOU WISH YOU KNEW THEN?

Now here we are. I guess it's 30 years later.

Seems like yesterday, but it's 30 years later, and having done this for all those 30 years in different roles and much more, being much more responsible for everything, I can talk about three different things I'd like to, there are three different things I'd like to talk about there.

First thing is, you know, I thought I saw the whole picture back then, but I didn't, okay? I saw what was affecting our little world.

So I think one of the things I've learned is that you need to *learn to see that whole big picture, take that 50,000-foot view.*

Don't get sucked into the tactical end of the operation.

It's okay to take a quick foray into, you know, into the tactical part just to get good at, say, as to what's going on. But you gotta quickly get back, step back, and make sure you're always, you're lookin' at that big picture at all times.

Second is, you need to understand, the understanding that I don't need to know all the answers right away.

You know, *the sooner I can visualize what the end stage should look like, the easier it's gonna be for us to get there,* but I shouldn't, I don't necessarily need to know that answer right away. I need to first, you know, *get my hands around the problem before we can solve the problem.*

So, and then the last thing about what I would wish I'd known then is, the biggest thing I've learned is *understanding that we didn't create this problem, but it's our duty to do our best to solve it.*

Sometimes that means takin' that step back to get the big picture. Excuse me. And this will aid in gettin' us to that end-stage quicker.

Sometimes *taking time saves time*, you know. It's very hard, and in my opinion, this was probably the hardest thing for me to learn as a crisis manager, is takin' that time to step back and let things slow down, and get a better handle of what's goin' on before I jump in with both feet and take control.

So, those are probably the three biggest things that I wish I had known back then.

#4 - WHAT ADVICE WOULD YOU GIVE SOMEONE WHO WANTS TO IMPROVE THEIR CRISIS LEADERSHIP?

Okay, so I love this question because I do this before I retired, I would have this conversation with every brand new lieutenant that would work for me. And sometimes even with new captains who came from other areas if I saw a need to have it.

And I tell 'em three things, three things that I expect from them. And if they do these three things, first of all, I'll stay off their back. But I think it'll help them become a better leader.

The first one is: *do not be afraid to make a decision.*

Trust your training and your instincts. You're in this position because you earned it. And I'm going to support you with whatever decision you make. I will not be there when you're making some of these decisions, and I may ask you, later on, why did you make it? And it may become a learning moment, and I will tell you to look at other things. But I will always support whatever decision you make. As long as you're gonna make it. A bad decision is probably better than inaction. At least you're trying to do something. So I tell them do not be afraid. I'm never gonna come down on ya, so.

Second thing I tell 'em is: *make sure you communicate clearly in all directions.*

And this is a little more complicated than it sounds. Because the first thing I tell them is to make sure your subordinates fully understand the directions you're giving them. We take for granted sometimes that guys understand what we're saying, and they really don't. Especially as a new boss coming in. So make sure they understand what you're telling 'em. Make sure you understand the directions that you've received from your superior. If you don't understand, ask questions. We think we all talk the same language, but sometimes, sometimes we don't, it's that simple. Sometimes I'm saying something, and I know what I mean, but you have no idea. So if you don't know, ask for clarification. And the third part that part of the communication is making sure the information you're reporting back. Okay, and the third part of that communication issue is making sure the information you're reporting back is clear and fully understood by me or whoever you're reporting to. And you'll find out very quickly if I don't understand what you're saying because I'll ask the questions. And you'll find out once the younger lieutenants and captains find out that you're gonna ask questions they're not afraid to ask questions of you either.

And the third thing I tell 'em is: *don't be afraid to be the boss.*

Embrace it.

Do it well, and you're people will respect you for it. And they, in turn, will have confidence in you and your abilities when you are in a time of crisis. The time of crisis is not the time to establish your leadership. And the fact that you are the boss. The sooner you do that, the better off your going to be, and sooner the men will be willing to listen to you and respect you and do exactly what you ask of them.

Especially in a time of crisis.

#5 - WHO IS A CRISIS LEADER THAT INFLUENCED YOUR CAREER?

Okay, so I'm going to answer this a little differently, also.

And I will get to one person who I think, but first I have to state, I've worked for many great crisis leaders and it would be hard for me to pick just one. And I really thought long and hard about this last night, and I did come up with one.

But from early on in my career, I had one of my lieutenants who said, "Look at all your bosses. "Emulate the best qualities of every one of them. "You don't have to do everything they do, "but pick out a quality from each one of them "that you think works and try and use that for yourself."

He says, "The first one you should try and learn is, "the first thing you should *realize is, "all people are motivated differently.* "And some bosses don't know how to motivate everybody, "and other bosses do."

He goes, "So the first thing you gotta do "is figure out how they're motivating their people "and what they're doing differently from other people "that can't get the people motivated."

So, I've used that throughout my whole career.

And, like I've said, I've worked for, I'm gonna say probably hundreds of good crisis leaders. And I've been friends, good friends with about four of five of our chief of departments, so and our staff chiefs and everything, so I've been good friends with a lot of good leaders.

And I'm going to say some of my best leaders were probably early on in my career, the battalion chiefs and stuff that I worked with as a fireman and as a lieutenant and captain.

But if I had to pick one, and because the question asked me to pick one, I'm going to go all the way back to my captain when I was a firefighter in a ladder company.

He had all the qualities that I spoke about in question number one, about what is a crisis leader. He also showed me how important a captain's job was in the fire department.

As a captain, and I didn't realize it at the time, but I realized it when I *was a captain, you have the opportunity to get all the new firefighters coming on the job headed in the right direction.* You are their boss. You are, to them, you are it. They report to you, anything you say, they're gonna do. They feel that their career hinges on your direction. And it does. I mean, if you sent them off in the right direction, they're good. If you don't set that good example as the captain and we have a lot of guys, in my opinion, who don't do this.

But, like I said, you have the most influence on the young people in the job, as the captain. I was fortunate to work with this great captain who I tried to emulate throughout my career.

He was probably the calmest individual under any type of duress that you would ever see. He treated everybody equally. He had respect for everybody. Even the bosses that he didn't like, you would never know it. And there were some. And I think part of that factor was that he was so calm and cool that some of the bosses almost thought he didn't care. But he, honestly, truly cared for everybody that worked for him. Probably, and the biggest thing I picked up from him was he was a gentleman for everyone.

So, I'm gonna have to say that he probably had the most influence and the fact that I still look back to the way that he acted and his influence on me. I hope that some of the guys that work for me will do that later on in their careers. So.

KEY TAKEAWAYS

- Don't take things personally
- Be calm, even-tempered and keep your emotions in check
- Be courageous, decisive and look at the big picture
- Listen to others, including those with an opposing view
- Never make a promise you can't keep
- Always protect your people, including from themselves
- Risk a lot to save a lot

- Make decisions based on what's best for everybody not just yourself
- Stay focused on the big picture
- Visualize what the end stage should look like
- Do your best to solve the problem even if you didn't create it
- Always give an honest answer
- Taking time saves time
- Do not be afraid to make a decision
- A bad decision is better than inaction
- Communicate clearly in all directions
- Don't be afraid to be the boss
- A crisis is not the time to establish your leadership
- Remember that all people are motivated differently

JOE MONROE - CHIEF OF POLICE – UNIV. OF KENTUCKY

Home	Lexington, Kentucky
Then	Chief of Police - University of Kentucky
Now	Chief of Police - University of Kentucky
Contact	**LinkedIn:** joe-monroe-58612a124/
Quote	*"Keep learning throughout your leadership journey ..."*

WHY JOE IS A CRISIS LEADER

Joe Monroe has earned the title of a crisis leader every step of his journey so far.

And unlike some people that reach the apex of their careers by crawling over others, Joe's legacy includes a wide and deep wake of other devoted, competent, and successful leaders that he has cultivated along the way.

One of the other factors for Joe's success as a crisis leader is the extraordinary network of other crisis leaders and other resources that he actively maintains. It's a rare moment when he doesn't have a relationship with someone to help in virtually any situation and even more rare that those contacts wouldn't drop everything to help Joe.

Joe's willingness to share what he knows to anyone who asks epitomizes his role as a crisis leader who is committed to leaving a lasting legacy.

His focus on leaving a useful legacy made such an impact on me that it inspired the name for this book project.

Thanks, Joe.

#1 - WHAT IS A CRISIS LEADER?

So, what I feel like a crisis leader is somebody that can step into a role at a moment's notice and manage a critical incident.

So that *takes a lot of skills plus it also takes a lot of education and experience.*

But more importantly, it's somebody who is very able to think very quickly on their feet.

By thinking very quickly on your feet, you're able to process things at a rapid pace more than somebody that's not a critical thinker.

#2 - PLEASE SHARE AN EXAMPLE WHEN YOU RELIED ON YOUR CRISIS LEADERSHIP?

Probably an example that I could use to talk about a time when I really had to focus on crisis leadership is recently here, we've had an incident that involved a father and his two sons who were leaving a football game, and upon leaving the football game before it was actually over, they were leaving early, and they were struck by a drunk driver where all three were injured, and the three-year-old little boy was fatally injured.

His injuries were catastrophic, and they resulted in the ultimate death of the individual.

So when you look at the leadership on that critical incident, we first had to look at how to secure the scene after we got the safety for the scene taken care of, but we also looked at, of course, the injured were already transported immediately to the hospital.

When I got to the scene, one of the things I noticed, there were shoes lying in the street, but I also noticed a young boy sitting on a porch that was crying and a woman, who appeared to be the resident of that house, was consoling the young boy.

That ended up being the five-year-old brother of the deceased three-year-old. The shoes actually belonged to him.

So he was hit as well and lost his shoes, and his father had already been transported, his younger brother had already been transported with the injuries.

So my first priority was to secure the scene and then take the young child, the five-year-old child, and reunite him with his father and his mother, who was on the way to the hospital.

So that was that first life safety priority in a crisis.

The second was securing the scene and then starting the process of evidence collection and getting that whole initiative moving, with calling in the resources from our partners to make sure that they were properly documenting the scene because we knew it was going to be a fatality.

The third piece of that is, as this was unraveling, the game started ending.

This was a major traffic route for us, for our exit, so we immediately had to contact our command posting and come up with an alternate traffic management plan to reroute this traffic away from this road now that it was closed because of it.

We actually put out messaging of a critical incident that involved a fatality, so we could make sure that people understood why we were closing the roadway and reduce the negative impact that we were going to receive for closing that.

We received no negative feedback from that, altering that traffic plan.

So that was probably one of the most forefront that I can recall in my memory of an example of crisis leadership that you had to put a lot of the skills you learned, a lot of the stuff we talked about in an emergency, special event planning, all come to fruition very quickly.

2.1

Another piece to that whole situation was post-event, we had to look at doing critical incident stress debriefing for our team, including myself, where we were processing the death of this child and the impact it had on us, 'cause we all had small children that age.

When you have officers who are performing life safety CPR on a three-year-old, trying to save his life, and realizing that he is going to be a fatality, that plays a heavy toll on first responders.

So that was a critical component that evolved into this whole thing, in the end, is, you had to focus on the crisis leadership and to *make sure that you looked at the human piece of it and getting that mental health.*

#3 - WHAT DO YOU KNOW NOW THAT YOU WISH YOU KNEW THEN?

You know if you stop and think about it as you evolve through a career, you always look back, and you're like, gosh, I wish I had known about this or that long before I'm at the point I am now because it would have made you a better leader.

So one of the things that I think is important to look at is that the journey you make in a career depends on identifying the journey in other people's careers, the experiences that they went through, and you learn from them.

You take the knowledge that you learn and apply it to your career.

To say, okay, I don't want to make that mistake that this chief made or this fire captain made, or whoever.

So you're identifying these critical points that you can learn from and not make those same mistakes, and I think that's probably one of the most important things you look at.

I look at a lot of things from leaders going all the way back to Abraham Lincoln, things that people are like, well that doesn't really apply to modern-day, but the principals actually do.

That's the whole thing, that you look and evaluate the whole totality of the circumstances, what you can take out of it and apply to your current experience as you move forward in your journey.

#4 - WHAT ADVICE WOULD YOU GIVE SOMEONE WHO WANTS TO IMPROVE THEIR CRISIS LEADERSHIP?

So when you start to think about what would I tell somebody, a young chief, or a crisis leader, in a position that they're up and coming. What advice would I give them to be a better leader as they evolve?

Probably the first thing is to *identify your weaknesses*.

Identify what your weaknesses are, focus on them and how you're gonna improve them. Whether it's learning from a peer, a mentor, or seeking out that training that's going to make you that better leader.

One of the things that I did in my journey was I always looked at five to 10 years out.

I never focused on that zero to five because by the time you are looking on the zero to five years is already gone.

So you have to be ahead of yourself and look at five to 10 and 10 plus out. And that's kinda the way that I structure our organization.

As a chief, I'm focusing on ten years out or more.

I want to develop these young leaders to be critical thinkers and handle critical situations by giving them the resources they need, the training they need and let them apply it and have those real-life experiences.

Because even if you take it and do it in a small format, for a small event or an incident, they're gonna learn from that and be able to build upon it so that the day that a major event or incident happens they're gonna have that background and knowledge but they're also gonna have the confidence in themselves to do it.

#5 - WHO IS A CRISIS LEADER THAT INFLUENCED YOUR CAREER?

So, I don't know if I could identify, specifically one person, who probably influenced my crisis leadership skills for my career. I could probably name a couple.

Of course, you know, one of the first ones that are out there, it is Lincoln.

I mean, you know, Lincoln went through probably the most critical crisis in the history of this country, if not the world, and his philosophy, his skills, and then he continually learned as he went through, in his short presidency, and made the changes necessary.

But, probably more than anything, was he had the gumption or the ... confidence in himself, to make these critical decisions that were going to be unpopular, they were going to be not well-received, but they were the right thing to do.

And sometimes as a leader in a crisis, you've gotta do what's right for the situation, even though, partially, you may disagree with it.

You know, you don't like it, but you know it's what's best and what is the right answer.

So, that is one of the things you can see as you look and study Lincoln, that he did.

You know, there are others like, you know, Schwarzkopf, Colin Powell, they're more recent, but they all have great situations where they applied leadership skills and to crisis situations.

And it takes a lot for somebody to go out on a limb and make those decisions that aren't going to be well-received.

But, before you even get to that point of making those decisions, *you had to have built up enough respect in an organization that they're going to trust you*. The people around you, and above you, and below you are going to trust your decisions.

They're going, they'll look to you to make those critical decisions in a time of crisis, and they're going to feel good with it because they trust you.

Because, over time, you've *built those emotional and professional deposits, up in that bank account, sort of speak, and then when it's time to make those negative withdrawals, you're going to be in a lot more positive balance.*

But, that's probably the thing you gotta think about the most is that relationship building and making sure that you're preparing the people around you by showing them that you can do the job.

KEY TAKEAWAYS

- o   Know your weaknesses, so you know what needs improving
- o   Learn to think quickly on your feet
- o   Keep learning throughout your leadership journey
- o   Make life safety a priority during a crisis
- o   Leave a legacy for others to learn from
- o   Provide for your responder's mental health
- o   Focus on 10+ years out
- o   Think critically
- o   Build respect to earn trust
- o   Do what's right for the situation, even if you disagree
- o   Build up goodwill for future withdrawal

John James - Emergency Mgmt./EMS

Home	Russellville, Alabama
Then	Fire/EMS/Emergency Mgmt
Now	Instructor
Contact	**LinkedIn:** john-james-025b8811/
Quote	*"Make a decision and put it in place ..."*

WHY JOHN IS A CRISIS LEADER

John James is the reason that this interview project even exists.

After reading my first book, he suggested that there are people that would benefit from hearing more about what goes on in the mind of Crisis Leaders.

John was my first interview, and he blew my socks off with his stories about what he relied on to lead during a deadly disaster in his jurisdiction. Besides his lifetime of selfless public service, John is a Crisis Leader because he makes decisions and takes action while others are stifled by a pursuit of perfection.

I'm inspired by John's attitude about leadership, and you will be too.

#1 - WHAT IS A CRISIS LEADER?

Crisis Leader.

You know, of course, we know the formal term, but *when I think of a crisis leader, I look to people who're maybe not as defined as a leader or even recognized as a leader.*

It's the ability to formulate a response, a decision, an action, during a time of crisis, whether it's a personal crisis at home, or whether it's a public crisis you're a part of.

So in my role and in my experience through life, the people I've seen that I would define as crisis leaders are those who at a moment's notice can be taken from a state of readiness and rest to full action and from that be able to take the situation at hand, formulate a plan, and put the plan in motion.

And I think the key to that is, and I give you credit, Mike, I think I read this in one of your books, is *making a decision and put it in place. It may not be the complete answer.*

It may not be the complete appropriate answer, but I think the key of a leader is one that says, okay, let's start this, and we reevaluate as we go, and we make those changes.

Another quality, you couldn't get caught up in the emotions of what's going on.

Obviously, if you're from there, your hometown, such as one of my events, tornadoes in a small town, and a county like us.

When you've grown up here, everybody knows you, you know everybody, so there were names being given to me during the event of people who had been killed that I knew personally, knew the family, but at the same time, I had to look at that as a fatality, a casualty, and just another circumstance that was going on and had to still perform.

And so I think the good crisis leader would be those individuals who can *take the events, bring people together, be that person that sort of can be the coach of the team and bring them up and get them motivated.*

Get them set on the right path and put them in action. Put them in motion and then be able to adapt that, not be so stuck in your own ways that you can't go, hmm, that's not working. Let's change it and go in this direction.

So, to me, a crisis leader is that person, that can move at a moment's notice, make decisions, formulate a plan, put them in place, but reevaluate and adjust as necessary to accomplish a goal.

#2 - PLEASE SHARE AN EXAMPLE WHEN YOU RELIED ON YOUR CRISIS LEADERSHIP?

So thinking of an event that sort of, I could say, allowed me to demonstrate what I would anticipate as crisis leadership ... Alabama was struck on April 27th, 2011, with a series of tornadoes that moved through our state and more focused to me, moved through our county in northwest Alabama, and struck a small town of Phil Campbell.

A small town, the population probably 1250 people. About nine miles away from my home and being from this county, this area my entire life, most of those people, I know, know me, and they're a community that is protected by a one or two-person law enforcement division and everything else, volunteers, fire department, ambulance service.

Having been a career firefighter, prior to my move to emergency management, we worked closely with those people, and I knew that my department would be called out to assist.

So even without being paid, when I heard the events unfolding and that the tornado had actually touched down in that community, immediately responded to the fire department, went into the community as a volunteer firefighter with my department.

Began doing search and rescue operations, where we had done the things that we, unfortunately, hope we never read about, that it always happens to someone else.

I'm speaking of having to simply mark and step over or around, those that have lost their lives. Toting the injured out on whatever pieces of material from a house that's been blown away, that you can find to do that.

Hauling people from inside these neighborhoods that have been just totally devastated, in the back of pickups and on the back of four-wheelers out to ambulances and then having to use tractors and other means to actually move through areas and pick up the bodies and be able to haul them out to be cared for. So started the day in doing those events, immediately as response and rescue operations. Moved into the nighttime, the tornado struck in the afternoon.

And so I'm back in my role, if you will, I'm back in the game as a firefighter, and honestly, that's what I'm trained to do, that's what I knew to do, and so we were doing *that work as best as we can.*

Things sort of came to a slowdown point if you will; we felt like all of the immediate rescues had been completed. We knew there would probably be a lot of ongoing rescues and then, unfortunately, some recovery operations that would have to transpire.

During the night at some point, I don't remember exactly when and how long, that the mayor and council, the mayor of the town of Phil Campbell, the fire chief, police chief, the sheriff, and some of the county elected officials came to me and quite literally, tapped me on the shoulder. And I turn around and there stands these individuals and they looked at me in what one could only imagine as a broken leader, who was devastated at what had appeared to have occurred in their communities and obviously needing some guidance in where to go next.

What're our next steps?

And they literally tapped me on the shoulder, and their words were, you're the only person we know in this county that's ever experienced any catastrophic event of this nature.

And they were referring to my time that I responded to Hurricanes Ivan, Katrina, and other events on the Gulf coast. And so through conversations, it was determined that they just needed a road map of how to move forward.

They felt like they had people that were alive, gathered up, and moved to triage, and moved some on to the hospital.

They knew there were other operations. They knew there were unaccounted for individuals, and unfortunately, dead that was probably still trapped in the rubble.

But then, how do they even move forward past that?

I give them credit that even that night, they already recognized the fact that very soon we will move from gathering everyone who's been injured or killed, but then we've got to rebuild our town. People are expecting things, and they knew that, and they knew they had to reach out somewhere, to someone that could give them that guidance and that knowledge and maybe some experience and hindsight that they could use.

So I happily agreed to step into that role.

I met with them and laid out some game plans of what we need to accomplish, what things needed to be done. Even laid out some groundwork of how to approach the governor and the federal officials that I knew would be coming to bare assistance in that. And then immediately put together a structure that we knew, we thought would work.

And I had to be very poignant with them and say, for this to work, you've got to let me organize, you've got to let me put this together, and you've got to agree to adhere to what I put in place.

We can't be working over each other.

We're working with volunteers; people are going to be coming from everywhere because it's the nature of humans to wanna assist.

And so they agreed to that, without any real discussion. It was just, "you tell us what we need."

I took that a step further, and I think this maybe is one of those key points that I think that a crisis leader has to do is I took that a step further to these people who were the elected officials. The fire chief, the sheriff, the mayor, the police chief of the town, the chairman of the county commission. And I pointedly said to them, "you do not, I'm asking you to not do anything in reference to this event without giving me knowledge of it occurring, prior to you doing it." And I explained to them that the reason for that was, is that there are things that would unfold over the next course of days, and weeks, and months, that the activities we do today could influence those decisions, such as their revenue reimbursement.

And so when I used that aspect of it, and I sort of, you don't stick your chest out as that person, but when you know you have the experience, and you know you have the ability, don't be afraid to step up and take that stand with those people who we normally look to for that leadership, because sometimes the lowest among us are the most qualified to be in charge.

And we have to recognize that. I think that's another characteristic of a good leader in itself, whether that had to have been me, or if I had to look below me for someone else at the time.

So we did that, we organized, and so I think that was the first thing that I could relate in that event that was a *strong point for a good leader, a crisis leader, is to be willing to step up to those individuals and say, this is the way it's got to occur for us to be successful, and if you want me to do that then this is what I need from you,* and I got that.

The second aspect that I think was really key to this event being successful.

I had been trained in NIMS and ICS, and all of the abbreviations, the courses, that we could think of that's out there. And working in a career service and in hurricanes we had a lot of career people and it was easy for people to adapt to that organizational structure and you could throw out terms such as liaison officer, food unit leader, branch director of a rescue branch, and another one for a recovery branch or whatever you needed and people understood that.

They understood, where they'd fit in. But on the first day following the storm, we had 750 volunteers sign in to assist. We were still doing secondary, second-level search operations, looking for recovery, honestly.

And then other things started to occur.

So we started having the overwhelming support of people who wanted to bring food to that community, and they were bringing it all to one central point. We had people bringing in equipment to do debris clearance. Excuse me. Which I knew needed to be done, not just for the roads, but people's property.

But at the same time, it's one of those things, knowing we've got to manage this because we've gotta capture that debris amount because of reimbursement issues and things like that.

So trying to pull that group of volunteers together and organize them in a way, where this 10 or 12 people work with this one person, who sort of had what their mission was, or their task, if you understand, in mind. And I could send them out to a predetermined area, and they accomplished the work at that area, and they would come back and say, okay, we're finished here. Where do we go next?

And so I knew that was the challenge and so I found a few people that had a little background in various things.

Had one game warden, who had came and volunteered, he was still an active game warden. He was actually on leave to retire, he came and said, I'm here, what do you need? And you would think game warden, law enforcement, but what I knew, he had just returned from serving our country, I believe in Iraq. And there he served as, what they're titled, as a logistics officer. And so the movement of people, equipment, and resources was nothing new to him.

So I very quickly looked at him and said, hey, can you take a map of this area, divide it up into some grids, and I'm gonna have some people sent to you, and put them in teams and give them a work assignment, and can you coordinate that for me? He said not a problem, and so he did that.

Another example is, as I've said earlier, every church in our community, every civic group, stores, restaurants, anyone who prepared food, was bringing food to deliver to the community. And they were bringing it to the one structure that halfway withstood the events of the tornado, and they were bringing it to us, and that's where we were operating from, and it was overwhelming our facility.

One, the number of people was continually coming in, everybody wanted to talk and tell you their story, and you felt honored and obligated to listen because they had been through a horrific event. But at times then, it also, it sort of put chaos in our organization, and it lent to things getting out of control.

And so, there was a gentleman there who's wife was there and she's a very willing volunteer. A very capable person who will speak her peace, speak her mind. And I simply went to him and asked him, did he think she would mind if I gave her name to people who wanted to bring food and rather than put the food all in a central point, she identified some places around the town, that maybe we could get some pop up tents, and she could have these churches and these groups bring their food to that location.

So people that were sifting through the debris of their homes, trying to salvage, could simply walk down to the intersection at the corner, and get something to eat and not have to leave their belongings that are scattered.

And he said yes, and she comes to me and she said: "I am so thankful, thank you for finding me something to do." I never mentioned to that lady that she was the Food Unit Leader. I simply found a person that had a niche for something, and I put her in place.

I could go on and on about people. The town had a very unique sanitary system for their sewage, and it wasn't working properly. So we had to call in porta-toilets, and they put them all in one spot.

And again, how beneficial was that?

Then law enforcement starts getting phone calls of people not using those, using other means.

And so I tasked this young man, who I had seen moving around town in a Bobcat, moving debris for people, but I noticed he had a set of forks that would lift down and lift items. And so I tasked him, I said, would you mind doing this for me? Take you a map, work with, it was actually his dad, work with your dad, identify some places, and let's put some of these around town, and then mark that map, contact the vendor, and let him know, these are where they're at, and start scheduling random emptying and cleaning of those units for the next month. He said, "I'd love to do that." That was gone. He never really knew he was a Facility or a Service Unit director.

The logistics guy, he knew it, but I never called him my logistics officer, you know, logistics chief. I just simply did that.

So I think the key to our success and the key to what I would say to a crisis leader in these events is one, *know your community*. Know the area you're in. Adapt once you've learned professionally, formally, whatever means of education you have in your profession. Find a way to apply, to fit, the people you're working with. One solution does not fix everything. So find a way to make it fit.

I never drew a command structure up on the wall. We never had a command structure.

We had phone number lists that everybody had. We did have a little list that a few people would know if somebody called in and said, they wanna know about this, rather than come to me I said, have them call Ms. Joyce. Have them go to Mike. Whoever the person was.

So we had our communications plan. We had an information process, that when information comes in if it was obviously about food, it went to Ms. Joyce, but if it was something they couldn't understand or didn't know where to handle this, they brought it to me and asked me to assign where this went to.

And those things happened naturally.

Simply because we used people, we put them doing things that we knew needed to be done, and we have a little bit of guidance, and we let the processes develop.

Not by trying to say, okay, what is our process? We've gotta follow NIMS, and we've gotta fill all these boxes, but who's doing the job.

We had a PIO who voluntary showed up with his radio station in tote. Honestly, he had a command, a little mobile radio station and says, I will do your broadcasts, live broadcast every 20 minutes from here, any updates you want comes out.

People were taking him information, and without even asking, he would bring that information and say, before I put something on the air, I want your initials on the bottom of the paper, so I know you have approved anything I put out.

So if they were establishing a new food place to get food, they would write it on paper and take it to him. He had a way to get me to approve that.

So again, information flow was a process.

The PIO was established. The radio guy took his own process and put together an information plan for our public, and from there, we were able to broadcast numbers to call for assistance.

So I think that's some examples of how I took an event and made a crisis leader out of it.

#3 - WHAT DO YOU KNOW NOW THAT YOU WISH YOU KNEW THEN?

To be quite honest, I probably knew it then, or I know I knew it, I'd had exposure to it, but I'm gonna say *the planning process.*

And I know that's a very broad term we use a lot in training and in this business it's the planning process, and we had done a version of the planning process during the tornado outbreak there in our town, but we didn't define it like we needed to.

We didn't probably document it as well as we should have, and we didn't really lay out everybody's objectives and then their strategies and things that we now know, from watching other events unfold around our country, where we could have probably been a little more efficient.

Because the one thing that I had to sort of step back from this and I have gained from it is even though it was my hometown, my home county and the town next to me, even though it was my people, so to speak, being injured and killed and it was my people, the volunteers that were out there responding.

Even my daughter's sorority and the entire university athletic program under head coach Terry Bowden at the time brought nearly 300 of their student-athletes and sororities there.

So it was truly my people, but at the same time, we didn't leave anything there, and I had to realize that even though that was going on, I felt like I've got to be there every moment to keep this thing moving.

And I spent the large portion of every moment there for several, several days. I would go home only to shower, only to clean up, and right back out.

And so what I knew that I didn't do that I know now is had I really invoked the planning process into a formalized, documented format, then I think I would have felt more comfortable.

Because I had the people that I felt comfortable in leaving control or sort of in charge, if you will, but sometimes just sort of giving them that road map of this is what I want to do and I'm confident in you, but here's something to lean back on.

So we met every afternoon.

Late in the afternoon, we would meet as a group with sort of the key people involved in all these different things, and we sort of just did a *status update around the table of where we were, which would be our situational updates.*

And from that we'd gather, here's where we're at, here's what we need to accomplish. The first two or three days, we went 24 hours a day, then we had to back off.

Once we realized we had recovered all of the individuals, and now we were truly in the recovery phase, we went down to about, this was in April, we went down to about a 16 or 17 hour day. We didn't do 12-hour shifts.

We simply *worked because of the number of people that we had that we could put in leadership positions.*

So we would work those extensive days, then we would leave for a few hours and come back. Even with the overnight, there were law enforcement issues to be dealt with, power restoration issues, sanitary issues, food unit issues.

So we didn't really put a plan together that said, here's the nighttime needs that I feel like sometimes we left, because I would go back in the next morning and it would be, hey, we had to do this during the night, or we did this during the night and would I would ask why, there really wasn't a true reason, other than somebody just wanted to do it that way.

And it required us, sometimes, to have to back up a little bit.

And that's not uncommon, and I'm not saying that was wrong, except *had we given a little more defined path and expectations laid out a little better, I think they would have stayed on target with what we needed.* It didn't really set us behind very much at all, a little bit a time or two.

So I think the key thing that I would say to someone is: *use what we know works.*

We know following NIMS and having a command structure, and having that span of control, we knew that works as I shared previously. We *know the planning process works,* sometimes as cumbersome and as bothersome as it is to go to meetings, and sometimes as repetitious as the things occur as the days unfold.

But when we moved from rescue to recovery, we knew we had to get debris.

We knew we had to get power restoration.

We knew we needed to determine a plan for our schools, because this community, the school was gone. It destroyed the school.

 It destroyed the only doctor's office, the only pharmacy, and one of the two grocery stores were gone.

So we were immediately into, had to have medical services for these people because these people's homes were destroyed.

So we moved into that, but we really didn't lay out those as objectives with who's accomplishing it. What's going on, and where do we expect to be in 12 hours to measure ourselves?

We just said we gotta get this done, and somebody went with it, and we were constantly having to get updates.

So I would say to someone, *use all the tools in your toolbox* if they're needed, and understand that yes, a lot of times, and we do this in real world, a lot of times with the planning process, it's done verbally between two people talking or a group of people accomplishing, but when you get to a mission that's catastrophic or large enough that you're gonna be turning over things that you're doing, to other individuals and I think in my mind, that's the key.

If I could stay there from start to finish as I did when I was an officer in command of the fire, and I was there, and I could stay from the time we rolled up the first engine, until we rolled the last hose, then I was comfortable with not having to layout a planning process. I would meet with whoever was in charge of interior operations and other stuff. Here's the game plan, let's go do it.

But when I know I can't stay there for the duration, and there are different people going to come in and play a part in this process, then I think the importance is to document it so that you stay on task and then the second piece goes along with just the historical means of documentation and how sometimes that can even transition into some financial recovery.

And so I would just say, what I've learned from that is *use those processes that we know is there and implement those even in some rudimentary form. It could have been written on the whiteboard* every day and erased tomorrow, took a picture with our phone now, that's the way to do it, you know.

Accomplish what we need to on the board. If we didn't do anything but write objectives on the board, here's what we want to accomplish tomorrow when we come to work, and everybody can look at that board and know that that's there, and capture it, and then build from that the next day.

So I think that's the piece that I wished I have done more in-depth, but I will say this, even though we didn't do it and I wished we'd have done it better, it did not cause us to fail.

We did the things; we just didn't capture it as we should have.

#4 - WHAT ADVICE WOULD YOU GIVE SOMEONE WHO WANTS TO IMPROVE THEIR CRISIS LEADERSHIP?

When I think of ways to improve someone's leadership, if I was trying to mentor someone, the first thing is that, is if I was looking, it's finding someone to mentor you.

Find that individual that you can look at and determine that maybe this person, they understand this, and they can relate to it from my point of view.

It's easy for a young firefighter, I'll use as an example, it was easy for a young firefighter to look to Chief Alan Brunacini, who's the known name of the fire service in this country, who left us with a legacy, left us with wisdom and training that's beyond anything that most of us could ever imagine.

And some of his leadership styles that set the standards.

But at the same time, when you look at his department size and the things he was able to accomplish, it may not work in a rural jurisdiction with one station, ten guys, three a day.

So find that mentor that has been successful, that has proven themselves, but that you can take their style and move it to the scale you need it to move to.

At the same token, nothing says you can't find someone that's at a one station department and employ their practices to one that's 20 stations large.

So find that person, *find that mentor and then talk to them.*

Plain language. Just sit down and have conversations with them. Hey, how did you handle this specific thing, which is actually the conversation that I've had with individuals about hey, you know people need to know, how did somebody accomplish this? And don't give me the answer in the textbooks and don't give me the New York City answer, give me the answer that fits for me in rural Alabama, or any other country you can plug into that.

And so that's the basis of what we're looking at today.

And then, just totally immerse yourself into the profession, into the education of the profession.

We can't always just be the known leader. Sometimes people have that trait, I do think that leaders are born with a trait, with a characteristic, with ability, whatever you wanna say, that when given the opportunity, and when they choose to sort of pull that to their forefront, that it will take ownership and they will become known as a leader.

The expectation is there.

I'm very humbled in that, but I say that about myself, in that, I feel that I have immersed myself and I have trained over my 30-something years of training.

Both formal education, professional education, and I've found my mentors and those people. To the point that even small projects around my old town and community and civic things I get involved in, people look to me and say, hey, help us out with this. Get us in a path, get us set in the right direction.

A quick example of that is I was the dad that got chosen to be president of the Band Parents Association as my daughter entered her senior year of high school and so from that, we put together a large band competition and those of you that have children in the band and activities, understand that.

And so, it came time for that to be put together and organized for the year and yes I was president, and I could have very easily just reached over and asked somebody to head that up, but the school band director and people come to me and goes, hey, we want you to put this together for us. Because this was the second year they had done it, it was sort of a new thing. And so I laid that competition day out and those events leading up to that.

Again, using what I knew in command structures and span of control and different activities being accomplished. And she's now been out of school about eight years, and I served one year as that president, and they recently had that same competition, and it was neat to see that they had those individuals that each had those some job responsibilities that we laid out originally because the plan worked.

And so, if you are that leader, *don't be afraid to step up* and show yourself.

Now don't be the arrogant person that thinks they always have to be in charge, but when somebody needs to be, demonstrate why you're there.

It'll make you better, it'll make you efficient, and at the same time, it teaches a philosophy that we share with people, practice every day, the way you wanna play.

And so if I use my ability, if I use my skills in leadership, sometimes those don't come across as well in those gigs around home as they do in other places, in catastrophic events. They're not as accepted as well.

But if I use those as practice events, when I demonstrate those skills and I take on a project and be a leader, then when real-world happens, and that major event comes, then I've practiced my skills and I've learned from those skills, and I've fine-tuned areas of improvement and it makes me a better leader.

And then find that mentor. Find that person as I did early in my career, that I could look to for guidance in there, and then immerse yourself in the education.

#5 - WHO IS A CRISIS LEADER THAT INFLUENCED YOUR CAREER?

When I think about when asked this question, and I referred often to the person that I can sort of point to as really setting me on the path of where I am in leadership, I immediately point to an individual that was by the name of Mr. Bruce Baughman.

Mr. Baughman was brought to Alabama by Governor Riley from FEMA, to be the director of the Alabama Emergency Management Agency. Bruce had served in various roles in FEMA. He had put in an illustrious career, over, I think, 28 plus years. He had served in the Oklahoma City bombing, the first World Trade Center bombing, the Northridge earthquake. A lot of key level positions, Director of Operations.

A lot of response and recovery operations.

So from him, not only did emergency management in our state of Alabama just excel, but I learned an enormous amount of information from him.

He was kind enough to give me books to read where he had actually highlighted parts and put post-it notes in and he would say, you need to read up on this topic.

And many of those have come to fruition.

Things that I can lean back, that he gave me that insight to.

And so I point to him, I refer to him often, as I said, as the person who not only brought emergency management to the forefront in Alabama and he was director during Ivan and Katrina, and from the success we had there, that I was fortunate to be a part of.

So I look to him, and then I always publicly thank him for the opportunities he gave me to step up through emergency management.

So he is the person that I look to the most in this profession as guiding me along in my career.

KEY TAKEAWAYS

- Maintain a state of readiness so you can take action when needed.
- Document the process to stay on task.
- Make decisions and rely on a process, but also re-evaluate and adjust if needed.
- Bring people together.
- Build plans to pass on to future leaders.
- Do the best you can.
- Use all the tools in your toolbox.
- When leading, clearly state your expectations, including those with a higher rank.
- Cultivate those that may not normally be leaders.
- An imperfect process is better than no process at all.
- Seek out a mentor.

John Nowell - Los Angeles City Fire Dept.

Home	Thousand Oaks, California
Then	Los Angeles City Fire Department
Now	Retired
Contact	**LinkedIn:** john-nowell-1b24838a/
Quote	*"Maintain consistent tone and tempo ..."*

WHY JOHN IS A CRISIS LEADER

Before I met John Nowell, I heard about John Nowell. His reputation as a commanding, informative, and engaging leader preceded him.

And true to form, I completely understood and agreed once I had the opportunity to meet and work with him.

John's diverse fire-service career enables him to distill many complex topics into those that are simple and understandable. As a teacher, John is in a league all his own.

As a crisis leader, his presence provides comfort. So much so that his crews memorialized that sentiment in a plaque presented to John upon his retirement:

Your assignment, your spot,

The place where you chose to work.

We had you on all three platoons,

All three express now their gratitude …

You led by doing, teaching, guiding;

Exemplary all the while.

Ever approachable, quick to laugh,

First in offering yourself to any task

Or anyone in need.

We wish you God's abundant blessing!

And know that never ought be forgotten,

The comfort felt by those in the fight upon hearing

John Nowell says:

"Battalion 12's on scene …"

The relief his crews felt when he was in command is understandable.

From his quote about 'tone and tempo' to his answers to the below questions, you'll see that his consistent and authentic crisis leadership is why I wanted to share his story.

#1 - WHAT IS A CRISIS LEADER?

So we're gonna talk about what I believe to be the qualities of a crisis leader and I would tell you that from experience on the Los Angeles City Fire Department, invariably some of our best crisis leaders were those people who obviously provided those levels of leadership and experience that when things were at their worst invariably they were rising to the occasion and had the ability to lead a group of individuals into some very bad situations and more often than not the better leaders, crisis leaders, would have a positive outcome as a result of that.

How did they get there, and how did they develop that?

I would suggest to you that as you look around your department or your organization, invariably you are looking for *people who will almost always have an incredible level of experience that got them to that point that they could provide that level of leadership when you came into the crisis mode.*

I would also suggest that being a good crisis leader would be indicated by *your ability to be a good everyday, non-crisis leader* and invariably it's those people who have the experience and the knowledge and have made the time and the effort in not only training and preparing themselves but making a dedicated effort at training the people that work with and for them over the years to also be able to perform at a very high level when the crisis does occur because there are probably *two different types of crisis leaders, those who are successful at mitigating incidents and those who in and of themselves occasionally have the ability to create or worsen a crisis. And those can almost always be spotted by their ability to lead on a day to day non-crisis mode.*

So I would suggest to you that historically, especially on the Los Angeles City Fire Department those people who have the experience and quite often as I went through my career I would try and identify those people who literally intimidated me and ask myself why do they intimidate me and invariably it was because of their experience over the years, their having been to a multitude of incidents, their experiencing in managing people on a day to day basis, and their commitment and their efforts to not only make themselves better but also the people around them, their ability to recognize that being successful and managing a crisis did not fall on the one single person in charge of that particular crisis but was gonna fall upon everyone that was involved in that same incident and therefore they are always gonna make sure that the people that are working with and for them are trained to the highest ability they can be in order to be successful in every aspect of that particular crisis.

We also know that certainly in the fire service, a great deal of our *ability to be successful is our ability to recover.*

It is probably more rare than common that we go to an incident with some preconceived notion of the outcome only to find that the fire and or mother nature had a different idea for us so we are constantly having to regroup, recover, and adjust our abilities and a good crisis leader has the ability to recognize that and has the ability to work with and convince their people that are working there that it is the right thing to do to go to an alternate method.

The other thing we notice in our better leaders of course is that their ability to lead in a non-crisis phase which is 99% of a career, of course, doesn't change when the bell goes off, and you go out the door and you're challenged with a massive incident that what I affectionately like to call their tone and tempo changes very little when they're going from the non-emergency day to day management to all of the sudden being faced with a very large what is perceived to be a crisis by certainly Mr. and Mrs. Smith who made the original 911 call so that as you go to an incident, and you're working with your *people they know and recognize the calming effect that tone and tempo by an experienced leader can provide in order to successfully mitigate an incident and they appreciate that.*

You can imagine as you're going out the door of a fire station and all of the sudden the messages start coming over the radio that you have a significant working incident that the adrenaline rush is incredible, and you will have all levels of that adrenaline rush and all levels of reaction to that rush based on the experience and the level of training that everyone responding has.

So they're *always looking for the leaders amongst us who are gonna be able to maintain that appropriate level of tone and tempo to bring some calmness*, if that's even possible, in these situations.

Quite often we find that the more *successful people in that process are the ones who recognize the capabilities of everyone that's working with and for them, they have made a dedicated effort to train them, they have the experience that they have been there and done that* and every position that's gonna be operating at the incident, and therefore they are not getting on the radio and asking for arbitrary, unnecessary information on a regular basis because having been there and done that they know what every one of those individuals is up against at the moment and they recognize that it takes time in order for them to be successful in every one of their specific operations that you assign.

So the more successful crisis managers recognize that and rather than *asking questions constantly throughout, which is by the way probably a prime indicator of their lack of experience*, because of their experience there is a tone and a tempo on the radio that is calming and allows them the opportunity to be successful and more often then not you are providing them information from your outside clear air view on whether or not it is obvious they are successful in their efforts.

And if you've been there and done that in every one of those positions you know what they're going through, and you know that as they're crawling through a burning building or they're running a chainsaw or chopping with their ax on the roof, they don't have time and don't need to be bothered with asking mundane questions to the incident commander.

Our better crisis managers recognize that and provide them the opportunity to be successful and the information they need in order to determine whether or not they're successful as the clock continues to tick.

Always reminded of folks like Sully Sullenberger and the infamous Miracle on the Hudson where they were faced with literally one minute, and I believe about 39 seconds, to make some decisions in order to ditch their plane in the Hudson

River and I can always recall him afterward reminding us all that his *success was based on his 40 years of training and experience and not a day went by that he didn't make an investment in his training.*

Never conceiving that 40 years later he would make the ultimate withdrawal from that training account and in a minute and 39 seconds he did not rise to the occasion, he truly fell to the level of his training which fortunately was exceptional amount of training and ultimately ended up in the most successful ditching of an aircraft in the history of aviation.

#2 - PLEASE SHARE AN EXAMPLE WHEN YOU RELIED ON YOUR CRISIS LEADERSHIP?

When it comes to incidents that I have been involved with where crisis leadership has been an issue, certainly I think back over my 35 years with the fire department.

And as I moved up into the supervisory positions, I recognized that I was incredibly fortunate to go to a multitude of different types and kinds of incidents that were literally across the board and had the opportunity to do those repetitively.

So I mean it's everything from a single-family dwelling fire to a high-rise fire, from grass and brush fires to major earthquakes, to major civil disturbances and not only just within our area but up and down the entire state of California.

So I will tell you that once again in my efforts to be the best that I could, in managing those incidents and managing those people, it was always foremost in my mind that *I'm not going to ask them to do anything or go somewhere that I hadn't done or been myself.*

And also once again had a successful outcome with having been there or done that, which I think is key.

Is that through your activity levels that you develop that, once again what I like to call that tone and tempo that people appreciate, that as things are potentially getting what we would describe as worse, and the anxiety levels are going up, that I would actually make a conscious effort to *make sure that my tone and tempo were remaining consistent and had some level of calming as a part of that.*

And of course, the big part of leadership is truly being out front and leading them through those capabilities.

So once again, having the opportunity to go to a multitude of incidents in virtually every firefighting position gave me the opportunity to recognize what each one those individuals within the organization were charged with.

So that crisis leadership has truly an affair of everyone involved.

And everyone needs to be successful in order for the leadership to be successful also.

#3 - WHAT DO YOU KNOW NOW THAT YOU WISH YOU KNEW THEN?

So, what do I wish I knew then that I know now? Everything I just talked about.

Certainly when you're young in your career, I was incredibly fortunate to come into the fire service at a minimum age requirement, and as you can imagine, back then, if you're absolutely inexperienced, you don't know exactly what to expect and all of a sudden you're thrown into this environment of incredible professionals.

What I wish I knew then, that I know now is that I probably equally as accidentally or consciously, worked my way up through every position that was available and had the opportunity to work at many of the most, the busiest, and most successful areas and stations throughout the city of Los Angeles.

So, probably unbeknownst to me, I was receiving the training and education of how best to do each one of the positions that I held, and I got an incredible amount of recognition, prime decision-making experience, on how each one of those positions should react and operate in a multitude of different incident types.

So, of course, if I'd a known 45 years ago, what I know now, I would've made an even better and more *conscious effort to identify those areas where I'm gonna get the experience and those people who I'm gonna get a positive experience from.*

And I would suggest to you that almost immediately within the beginning of your career, those folks will be identified and they're more often than not, those who are intimidated by other folks on a job.

And all you need to do is make sure that their intimidating for the fact that they are incredibly successful and experienced in what they do, not for any negative reasons.

And if you search out and go work for those folks who have that intimidation and that experience going, well then your organization, invariably, you can't help to become better and better prepared as you go throughout your career and you'll be far more successful in your endeavors.

#4 - WHAT ADVICE WOULD YOU GIVE SOMEONE WHO WANTS TO IMPROVE THEIR CRISIS LEADERSHIP?

My best advice to someone interested in improving their crisis leadership is that you have to make a conscious decision to put yourself in those positions that are going to force you to become the best that you can be in your position.

I will tell you, and I probably didn't recognize it, in fact I know I didn't, earlier in my career, because you don't think of those things, but what I found myself doing was identifying the busier places to work so that I could go to more, bigger, more intense incidents and work invariably with those folks on our department who were leaders in each of those areas because they had a tremendous amount of experience and especially positive experience in going to those multitudes of incidents.

So you need to make a conscious decision to go work where you're going to be busy, and you're going to be immersed in the process.

What I ultimately learned in my training positions in the department was that there is *a process called recognition-primed decision making*, and I finally realized that's exactly what I had been involved with throughout my career.

I had gone to a multitude of incidents, many times over, and had a multitude of different experiences, so I was able to *develop that slideshow of having been to all those different incidents and recognizing what the outcome should be.*

And I think it's also important that when you go to those locations, and you immerse yourself in all those different types of experiences that you're doing it with those *experienced leaders who have had a successful outcome, not those ones who maybe have a less than successful outcome which could almost be described as crisis creators.*

So, I think it's important that you immerse yourself. And quite often, what I found myself recognizing is I was looking for those places to work and the people to work with who had intimidated me, who have reputations on the department for being positively aggressive, with a positive outcome as a result of a multitude of incident experiences.

And those are the ones that I tried to gravitate towards.

I also recognize that it wasn't just the leaders in each of those locations that needed to provide me those experience, but those leaders reside throughout the organization at every level right down to, and especially including, the basic firefighter level and working with those firefighters who have a tremendous amount of experience and what we affectionately describe as the *locker room leaders of an organization who have that experience and that intelligence and that calming effect that when things are at their worst*, they have been there, they have successfully done that, and they will safely get you through that experience so that you can develop that into another slide of your experience carousel as you develop throughout your career.

#5 - WHO IS A CRISIS LEADER THAT INFLUENCED YOUR CAREER?

So when we talk about those folks who have influenced you over the years, I think that influence truly works both ways.

Certainly, what you want to do is put yourself in places and positions to get the positive influence or the positive outcome at the most number of incidents that you could possibly go to.

Conversely, I can't help but recall that throughout my career, there were also folks who provided me with the opposite of that.

So that I would also put that into my slide carousel, that in certain situations, I wanted to make sure that I didn't react or overreact in a method that some folks have a tendency to do.

And that's probably that negative leadership, negative crisis management, that you want to be involved with, so it works both ways.

So I think you have a conscious decision, and you have the ability to put yourself in places and positions and surround yourself with people to provide you the positive experience, and that is exactly what you have to do.

And again, I think you need to do that within every position within your organization from the bottom all the way to the top.

And recognize who it is that you want to work with and how they're going to influence you from the basic positions within your organization to the leadership positions.

We are incredibly fortunate, as you can imagine, we have every level of that experience and some cases intimidation within our department, and as long as you're utilizing the positive examples of that, you're going to be certainly better prepared.

So it's a matter of working for and with those people.

Immersing yourself, especially in training. There is no alternative for immersive training and preparing yourself and your people, and providing your people with the training opportunities they need to be successful is your only hope for being a successful crisis leader.

They have to be successful every time the bell goes off in order for you to be successful. We have some incredible examples in the Department.

We have a gentleman who coined our training model of *"Train as if your life depends on it because it does."*

And that has been our mantra and certainly my mantra throughout my career as I prepared myself.

Again, I made the effort to transfer to and immerse myself with those leaders who had intimidated me, when almost immediately you recognize that if you're there for the right reasons and if you're there to immerse yourself in training and make yourself a better person, then they are going to embrace you and they are going to carry you with them along with their successes.

And that is exactly what I was able to do is work for some of those Captains and those Chiefs who had that capability and would literally live and dwell in the training environment.

And it also became very obvious that *when you live and dwell in the training and preparation environment, those other issues that have a tendency to rear their heads in the non-emergency environment have a tendency to go away.*

Because everyone that comes and wants to work with you has that same mantra of wanting to become better at what they do, so when someone calls and the bell goes off, *we are going out and providing the highest level of service we possibly can.*

And that's where we dwell throughout our careers.

KEY TAKEAWAYS

o   We always fall to our highest level of training
o   Successful leaders manage their tone and tempo

- Only ask of others what you have done yourself first
- Be a leader every day to be a good leader during a crisis
- Everyone needs to be successful for the leadership to be successful
- Seek a position that challenges you to be your best
- Recognize your organization's the 'locker room leaders'
- Build a slide show of experiences to draw upon
- Live and dwell in a training and preparation environment
- Learn from both positive and negative leaders
- Seek out positions and people that will give you experience while avoiding crisis creators
- Invest in your training every day
- Being successful requires our ability to recover
- Immerse yourself in training
- Work and learn from people that are intimidating (from having immense experience)
- Train as if your life depends on it because it does
- Provide the highest level of service possible

Jonathan Bernstein - Crisis Management

Home	Monrovia, California
Then	US Army Intelligence; Stuttgart, Germany
Now	Strategic Leadership in Crisis Management
Contact	**LinkedIn:** crisismanagement/
Quote	*"Trust your intuition ..."*

WHY JONATHAN IS A CRISIS LEADER

Jonathan and I first met as regular contributors of an online TV show called "The Crisis Show," where we would discuss a topical crisis event that was extensively covered by the news media.

Those appearances were colored by Jonathan's well-developed sense of humor and witty repartee. Needless to say, we hit it off immediately.

Of course, his role in extracting and sharing his keen insights into the crisis also proved to be phenomenal. Jonathan is a seasoned crisis leader in part because of his pragmatic and informed approach to navigating his clients through even the thorniest of crises for over 30 years.

Chocked full of helpful lessons, I'm pleased to able to share some of Jonathan's stories here.

#1 - WHAT IS A CRISIS LEADER?

So first, Mike, thanks for asking me.

A crisis leader really is someone who can keep his head when people are shooting at his feet literally or figuratively.

In the military, they call that situational awareness.

It's the ability to think intuitively and quickly and kind of jump from point A to point L sometimes without necessarily working out the steps in between.

But I think a crisis leader is also *someone who inspires this organization to build crisis preparedness and crisis response best practices right into the fabric of the organization*.

#2 - PLEASE SHARE AN EXAMPLE WHEN YOU RELIED ON YOUR CRISIS LEADERSHIP?

So, I was in the military for five years, and I was originally trained as a military cop, and before I got into military intelligence work.

I was on routine patrol of a military housing area in the Stuttgart area in 1974 or so, and I suddenly saw smoke coming out from the local high school and drove my Jeep right over there, and there were people streaming out of the building.

There was black smoke coming out of the building; basically, a lot of chickens with their heads cut off.

The fire department was not there yet. German Fire Department served the housing area, and they had not yet arrived.

So I went in and tried to take control of the situation because nobody there was, and I was able to direct people to evacuate.

I was actually able to find the source of the fire, which was a couch that students had set on fire in a stairwell as a senior prank, and I managed to heave the couch out a big plate glass window, and that took care of the stairwell.

So at the end of the day, I basically played firefighter as a cop, but we were able to identify some suspects, nobody got hurt, I got a lot of smoke inhalation but I found that I had a knack for leading in a crisis that, you know that *was the first time I had really tested that and it motivated me to do more of the same.*

#3 - WHAT DO YOU KNOW NOW THAT YOU WISH YOU KNEW THEN?

One thing I wish is that I knew then I could make a good living telling other people what to do when the shit hit the fan.

I didn't know it was a career at that point, but apparently, it was.

But more seriously, that was one of the first times that I really trusted my intuition in a dangerous situation.

And I wish it didn't take me as long as it did to start to really *trust those inner voices.*

Probably took me decades before I fully trusted my intuition, and that's a critical skill to refine if you're going to be a crisis leader.

#4 - WHAT ADVICE WOULD YOU GIVE SOMEONE WHO WANTS TO IMPROVE THEIR CRISIS LEADERSHIP?

Well, basically *people should learn to listen, and they should learn to learn, and they should learn to practice.*

And by listening, I mean listening to the people who you lead, and ask them for feedback on your leadership skills.

If you can't have transparent communication, you're never gonna know when you're going a little bit off track, or discouraging people, or encouraging people.

And also, learn more skills of the type necessary to be a good crisis leader. We're not born with all of them.

And there's plenty of training available out there.

And then practice that, with workshops, and simulations of various kinds.

But also, as I'd mentioned in an earlier *question, this whole idea of intuition* is a skill set in and of itself.

I think everybody's intuitively born with a certain degree of intuition, and there are all kinds of psych tests which test your intuitive abilities.

But whatever your level of intuition is, it can be refined.

And it's *learning some unusual business skills, like meditation,* learning how to get to that quiet place inside of you where your intuition resides. And there's a lot of paths to get there.

But I think that you'll find that a great many crisis leaders have learned to do that.

#5 - WHO IS A CRISIS LEADER THAT INFLUENCED YOUR CAREER?

Strangely enough, in one brief moment in our history, I put a crisis leader on a pedestal from which he later fell rather hard. And that was Rudy Giuliani. His performance as a crisis leader on and about 9-11 was phenomenal.

It was the epitome of what I later dubbed the three rules of crisis communications ... the need to come across with *compassion*, *confidence*, and *competence*.

He really demonstrated all three of those consistently during the early days of that crisis. Unfortunately, he's gone off on a very weird tangent since then, and tried to sell himself as a crisis manager at one point, but that didn't work out.

But in the moment, he was the guy who could reach that quiet place and lead, and he did it very well, and that was inspirational to me.

KEY TAKEAWAYS

- o Communicate with compassion, confidence, and competence.
- o Learn to listen, learn to learn, and learn to practice.
- o Test your leadership under real or simulated conditions.
- o Trust and refine your intuition.

o   Build crisis preparedness best practices into the fabric of
        your organization.

o   Refine your intuition through meditation and other non-
        traditional business skills.

KEN WALTHER - EMERGENCY MGMT/RAIL INDUSTRY

Home	New York City area, New York
Then	Lead Transportation Manager
Now	Emergency Management/Rail Industry Professional
Contact	**LinkedIn:** ken-walther-176b5458/
Quote	*"Always improve the tools in your toolbox ..."*

WHY KEN IS A CRISIS LEADER

Leadership skills and humility go hand in hand, and Ken Walther has plenty of both.

While he is the last person to beat his own drum, when Ken speaks, people perk up.

And even though he has years of leadership experience under his belt, it's also apparent that many of the traits he speaks about come to him naturally. Both personally and professionally, Ken embodies what we need from a leader during a crisis.

As a leader with extensive familiarity with both the public and the private sector, Ken draws from the best of both worlds to provide world-class leadership from his very full toolbox of resources.

#1 - WHAT IS A CRISIS LEADER?

Crisis leader, to me, is the person who has the ability to effectively reduce the duration and the impact of an extremely difficult situation. So, a lot of phrases out there, a lot of, a lot of anecdotal information.

One of the things that come to mind is someone that can remain calm, cool, and collected.

So if you take the opportunity to look that up in a dictionary, it really just references somebody who's not upset or not very bothered by things. And to me, that's a bad correlation. Because somebody who's bothered by, not bothered by things, can't utilize some of the tools that they have in their toolbox that are necessary to formulate an effective response to a crisis.

So what are some of those tools?

Some of those tools are things like critical thinking.

The use of critical thinking prior to an incident directly impacts our ability to respond to an incident. Need to think about, and so, what's a practical application of critical thinking?

Well, maybe understanding the ramifications that a decision will have on the outcome of an incident before you actually implement that decision.

Things like emotional intelligence.

Things like situational awareness.

And probably most importantly, is empathy.

Understanding how other people will view the impacts of your decisions on them from a personal perspective, as well as the perspective that they provide during an incident.

So to me, it's a crisis leader is somebody who can utilize all of the tools or whatever the appropriate tools are that they have in their toolbox.

#2 - PLEASE SHARE AN EXAMPLE WHEN YOU RELIED ON YOUR CRISIS LEADERSHIP?

A few years back, I was responsible for the operation of a major transportation network in New York City, specifically in charge of a terminal that was operationally in charge of a terminal that was fed by four tunnels.

On the particular night in question, there was a train in one of the tunnels that came across a fire, the source of which really, for this story, isn't necessarily important.

What's important to know is that tunnels that trains operate through are very tight, closed. The outline of the tunnel is close to the trains and produces what's called the piston effect as trains traverse through the locations. Well, the train in question came upon a fire, reported it to us in the operation center.

And one of the things that's tough to operate in a railroad situation is they don't have the ability to steer, so there are only specific routes that specific trains can take.

It was our effort to get to the train that was involved in the fire first. In the station that I'm talkin' about, there are trains that operate into these tunnels literally every other minute, so the five minutes that it took for this train to arrive on the scene, there were three other trains in behind it already that had left the station.

These places don't have a lotta room.

Smoke was building.

We brought the three following and then what, at least for this portion of the story, could be considered the incident train, got them back into the station.

But what's not immediately evident to people as they operate through these situations is there are other trains with other people on them, so in an adjacent tunnel, there was a train that was awaiting space in a station to actually land at the station and allow the customers to disembark.

Well, as we removed the trains from the tunnel with the fire and the smoke, they actually drew the smoke into the station area and into the tunnel where the train that I'm gonna talk about now was actually sitting.

So, the train in the tunnel about to arrive in Penn Station is now becoming flooded with smoke due to the incident in the adjacent tunnel. And while there is no immediate danger of fire or anything like that on the train in question, the smoke is really gettin' dense.

These trains typically have about a thousand people on board, this train a little lighter because it's in the opposing direction, so probably about 350 people.

I have an engineer on that train who now sees the station filled with other trains, meaning that there is nowhere for this train to arrive.

The smoke is building.

Panic starts to set in onboard the train.

And through the panic that this operating person is surrounded by begins to elevate their level of concern, to the point where they start yellin' on the radio that I need to get in, I'm ready to get outta here, and the smoke is rising.

You know, it's hard to, there are lots of tools available to us in a crisis. Being able to pick the right one at the right time is critical at any moment.

This was a case where, you know, radio traffic, hundreds of radio transmissions. You hear this engineer on the radio, the voice level, the inflection is rising.

To me, it created an opportunity.

The opportunity that I'm talkin' about is I went on the radio, cleared all of the other radio traffic that was goin' on, and actually utilized this instance to kinda violate a rule.

Many times when people are involved out in the field, they need to know that there are other people thinkin' about them, so I basically got on the radio, addressed the engineer by first name.

Said, this is Kenny. I know that you're out there, and I know the smoke is gettin' worse. What I need you to know, and what I need you to understand, is that we're workin' hard to create some room in the station to get you and your folks in, and out of danger. We understand that the situation seems to be gettin' worse in the field, but understand that in front of you, the situation is gettin' better, and it's just gonna be another minute or two.

I told her exactly what we were doin' to move other people around and move our other equipment around, and you could literally hear their answer, the change in their voice when they answered, like a breath of fresh air, no pun intended. Very calming, she understood. Answered me, said, Kenny, thank you so much.

And onboard the train, that translates to the customers that are surrounded by the same situation, right?

So, when you have a radio in hand, always remember that you're surrounded by other people and what you say and do isn't necessarily only received by the people that you're speakin' to on the radio. We tend to lose sight of that as well.

So the people that were in the car, where she was stationed, also heard me on the radio. And when I debriefed with her afterward, it had a calming effect not only on her and the other members of the crew but on the customers that were within earshot of the radio transmission.

People just need to know that you're thinkin' about them.

People just need to know that you understand the situation that they're in.

People need to know that you have empathy.

That's probably one of the biggest tools that you have in your toolbox when you are surrounded by the chaos that we are often surrounded by in these situations.

#3 - WHAT DO YOU KNOW NOW THAT YOU WISH YOU KNEW THEN?

The short answer to that question is everything. So let me explain that answer.

It's not that I know everything now, it's that I wish then I knew everything that I have been able to learn up to this point.

Really it's the answer to the question is about growth.

It's about being a continual learner and utilizing again the toolbox that I always reference. It's always putting things in your toolbox.

So whether it's a case study, whether it's a book that you read, whether it's speaking to another person who's involved in your industry and out, probably more importantly, outside your industry. It's *utilizing those learning opportunities to keep filling your toolbox.*

So I'll never know everything, but man, do I wish I knew then what I know now because there are tools that I have gleaned from other people that I could have applied in this situation and maybe not in the exact moment of time with the situation, situations ebb and flow, but maybe in my earlier response or maybe in my closure of the incident and documentation of the incident, maybe it's through some of the lessons, the principles of lessons learned and being a learning organization and implementing that throughout your organizational structure.

So what I know now that I wish I knew then, again, everything.

#4 - WHAT ADVICE WOULD YOU GIVE SOMEONE WHO WANTS TO IMPROVE THEIR CRISIS LEADERSHIP?

Someone that wants to improve their crisis leadership.

The best advice for that I can give is to *be a continual learner and to utilize opportunities that aren't always evident in your particular field.*

Yeah, one of the people that influenced me was an academic, and they taught me to utilize tools like the internet to pull information out from other genres and utilize information from other businesses.

So what would my advice be?

Either use the tools that are available to you in a non-traditional method or, because as leaders, we don't always have time to look up stuff on the internet or read case studies and do all that kind of investigative thing.

Maybe you hire somebody.

Maybe you give it to a member of your staff; the person that we hired was exactly what I described, an academic, actually at times in his career was an inspirational speaker.

I learned so much from that person from a non-traditional perspective.

So my advice to somebody who wants to improve their skill set is to *think outside the box and think outside the traditional lights and sirens kind of crisis intervention and identify opportunities to fill your toolbox.*

#5 - WHO IS A CRISIS LEADER THAT INFLUENCED YOUR CAREER?

The crisis leader that influenced my career the most is somebody who, in most circles, may not be considered a crisis leader.

He was hired by my organization to improve communications for, from a customer perspective.

What's important, in this discussion, is that he was an academic.

And he taught me how to research things or look at things from a completely different perspective than our traditional operations-based nuts and bolts perspectives. He taught me how to go on the internet, or the value of going on the internet, in, and utilize reporting and lessons learned from other organizations.

He actually helped me to create an entire 'lessons learned' section in our organization. He taught me the value of utilizing others' experiences and applying them to situations that may not be exactly the same.

Our influence doesn't always come from people that we're standing next to in the heat of battle.

Your influence can come from people who were standing millions of miles away, in a situation that was completely different.

I've learned lessons from leaders of commanders of navy ships.

I've learned lessons from people who were in charge of wildfire response.

I've learned lessons from people who were in charge of public relations firms, whose messages went out incorrectly.

The way that I've learned those lessons is to apply that academic approach. It is, to understand what the issue was, and the tools that these people, individually, utilized, in their specific situations, and then, through my critical thinking, apply those tools to the situations that I think may occur before they even happen.

So that you can formulate your response to things, and have, you know, we can't all plan for everything that's going to happen, right? But, through the thought processes of the academic world, situational awareness, critical thinking, emotional intelligence, all those things are of a piece in our response to events, that ultimately influence other people's thought processes and make us effective leaders in the field.

When people understand that we empathize with their positions, be they people that report to us, or people that are involved in situations beyond their control, when they know that their leadership has empathy, and can understand where their perspective lies, that their perspective lies in a response, that is a win-win, that I could never have learned, had I not, 'cause, we always don't have the ability for field experience.

So, we need to couple our field experience with those of the academics to understand and formulate an appropriate response.

So, my influencer probably has never been to the scene of a fire, or a crash, or anything like that, but has helped the people, has helped thousands of people, through events that I could influence the response to.

KEY TAKEAWAYS

- Stay calm, cool, and collected
- Think critically
- Include an academic approach to gaining knowledge
- Never stop growing as a leader
- Be emotionally intelligent
- Seek out inspiration and guidance from non-traditional sources
- Maintain situational awareness
- Demonstrate empathy
- Use the right tool at the right time
- Let people know you're thinking of them
- Learn continuously
- Think outside of traditional lights and sirens to solve a crisis
- Always improve the tools in your toolbox
- Include a non-traditional approach to learning

MIKE GIBLER - BATTALION COMMANDER, US ARMY

Home	Leavenworth, Kansas
Then	Battalion Commander, US Army
Now	Consultant
Contact	**LinkedIn:** michael-gibler-17479117/
Quote	*"Trust and empower your people ..."*

WHY MIKE IS A CRISIS LEADER

I've had the honor of knowing Mike for several years. During our visits, I've learned a little about his family, his insights on conflict, and what it means to be an American patriot in a foreign land.

One theme of our conversations centered around the significance we place on the symbol of our country ... the United States flag. Unlike most of us, though, he's had to drape the remains of his soldiers killed in battle in the US flag before sending the fallen home to their families.

So, like many of the leaders that I interviewed, Mike's *commitment to the service of an idea bigger than himself* was matched only by his commitment to serve the men and women he was responsible for.

As you'll hear, the clarity and resolve he has for these two principles are one of many reasons Mike is a crisis leader.

#1 - WHAT IS A CRISIS LEADER?

Mike, thanks for the interaction here.

The first question, as I understand it, that we spoke about is: What is crisis leadership?

A really complex problem, a really complex question, but I think the best way for me to kind of explain that is:

A crisis leader is someone who remains calm in an arguable environment that's difficult to do that in. Thinks clearly in that environment because a crisis can and does have a physiological and psychological effect on people, or at least stress does. Can they remain calm and think clearly through that? Then understand the end state that they want to achieve, not just as an individual, but organizationally what do they want to achieve.

How does this crisis need to end in their mind? Then be able to state that to the organization, to the response components as quickly as possible, and to achieve that as safely as possible. I think there are a few traits that equal this, and I'll just throw them out quickly.

You gotta set the example in all you do and where you do it. In non-crisis situations, that becomes a template for either how you should behave or how people believe you're going to behave in a crisis event, so you've got to set the right example at all times. You gotta understand your organization, you gotta know what it is, what its capabilities are, what its weaknesses are. You gotta understand the people that make that up and ensure that they are capable of responding in a crisis environment.

You gotta understand your role as the leader in managing the crisis, so that's kind of another trait that's out there.

The other piece I think that's important is that you can't start thinking about this at the crisis moment. You gotta *provide the necessary training upfront, and you've gotta provide people opportunities to fail before a crisis*. They're gonna succeed. If you picked the right people, it's a good organization, it's a good structure ... Naturally, they are succeeding, but you gotta put them in roles and environments where they can fail, or they do fail, but it's gotta be safe, they gotta believe it's safe, it's not judgemental.

You gotta get them outside their comfort zone, and you gotta provide them opportunities to fail, and as a leader, you gotta lead that by example. *You gotta admit where you fail, you gotta admit it publicly, and then you gotta better yourself, use yourself as an example to get folks to be willing to drive themselves to a higher standard.*

The other piece, I think, that's *exceptionally important, you gotta trust and empower your people.*

If your people are well trained and if you trust what they're gonna do, you trust that they understand their roles and their power to do it, it becomes really easy to manage a crisis, and you don't have all the burden on your shoulders, it's distributed across your organization. Kind of very easily, you gotta *provide them the resources, support, and direction*, if it's needed, again, only if it's needed to be successful during a crisis.

Then kind of on the back end of that, you gotta ensure that you as an individual, individuals involved in a crisis in an organization learn from that crisis. They've gotta 'after-action review' it, they've gotta take time to be retrospective and introspective about what they've done, what they did well, what they didn't do well, and they've gotta do that in a very forgiving environment. It cannot be judgemental, it can't be punitive, of course, unless something illegal, immoral or unethical occurred, but the only way you get better is to take a hard look at yourself. It's a long answer to a very, very short question.

#2 - PLEASE SHARE AN EXAMPLE WHEN YOU RELIED ON YOUR CRISIS LEADERSHIP?

Okay, what you've asked me in the second question is to share an example where I've relied on my crisis leadership. I'm not sure I can ...

Historically, I'm not sure I can reach back and say that was crisis leadership, it's just that I've got examples in which they were in interesting situations, and environments in which I've been in, and the organizations I've been in were involved in, and I believe my leadership played a role there.

But I'll harken back to a post that somebody I'd served with in the military put on his LinkedIn site, to discuss leadership. Really, to summarize it, I was in a ... It was an infantry organization, and I was an infantry battalion commander. We were in the middle of a pretty complex operation. Things started to go a little bit wrong, and within that context, I could listen to and hear the stress, and I think ... I wouldn't say confusion, but just the stress that some of the junior leaders that were trying to manage an increasingly complex event.

So, we deployed more resources, the company commander asked for additional resources outside of the company, so I deployed with the battalion Quick Reaction Force (QRF). But, I wanted to take an opportunity just to drop down to the radio frequency that the platoon leader operated on, and this is really him relaying the story, not necessarily me understanding that this was occurring in his mind during the time that I just dropped down, and that's generally not done.

You generally don't end up on a platoon radio net at my level.

But I just touched base with him, and asked him to give me a quick situation report, and asked him what I could do to help.

In retrospect, and he relayed this in a story, is that that calmed him; apparently, I have a tendency to be fairly calm in stressful environments.

Our organization would say that they generally knew when things were really bad when I was the most calm.

That, I think, matriculated down to him, and knowing that I was confident in what he was doing, I think it helped him. That I wasn't overly concerned, and I wasn't ... I had confidence in his training, and his soldier's training, and knew that they would accomplish the task exceptionally well, that things were just not coming at them in a manner that he had seen before. I think from my opinion, I'm not sure that I was thinking about leadership, I'm not sure I was thinking about crisis leadership at the time. All I was thinking about was that as a senior leader of the organization during a fairly stressful, complex time, it was my responsibility to inject what I could into that to make sure he understood that I trusted him. I trusted his organization. I trusted his skills, and that I was there to help if he needed it.

I think that that can calm an organization. I think it can give confidence to individual subordinate leaders. I would say this repeated itself a million times in Iraq and Afghanistan, not only in my organization but others, in which you had organizations that were well trained. You had young leaders that were good at what they did as long as they were allowed to do it, and that you were able to underwrite their mistakes. Because mistakes were made. But you did so in a way that allowed learning to constantly occur.

#3 - WHAT DO YOU KNOW NOW THAT YOU WISH YOU KNEW THEN?

What do I know now that I wish I would have known then? I think then is relative. Now, as a 55-year-old person, as a young Lieutenant in the Army, 21 or 22, significantly different experience base.

But one of the things I think over time, and it relates to my answer to the previous question is, the *impact a calming or confident demeanor can have on a situation*. And I think I knew this intuitively. I knew that because that's how I viewed strong leaders and people that I tried to emulate when I was growing up in the ranks.

As the *screamers, the yeller's, the people that seem a bit unhinged during the most challenging times, did not help the organization or the individuals in that environment understand what needed to be done,* move towards potential ways to solve the problem.

It really froze the organization and either decision making, kind of a pause or a fear reflex that somebody that's unhinged, somebody that's yelling at you. What am I going to be able to do, to be able to balance that?

So I intuitively knew that or at least intuitively, that's how I chose to lead. But it's not really until I received feedback from others that when I exhibited that, or when other people exhibited that, but more specifically when I did, the real impact it can have on an organization.

And arguably, it can be exceptionally freeing, exceptionally beneficial to an organization to realize that *calm demeanor, deliberate thought, deliberate actions, really can be an undertone. And can be a common thread throughout a very chaotic, very challenging environment.*

And I may get into this later.

It gets into how do we incorporate those types of stressors into people's lives, into people's work, into people's environments so they can get comfortable with that? So they can get comfortable with that stressed environment and not let the physiological or mental things that occur in a crisis.

Start making them either pull on different parts of their personality or overemphasize certain negative aspects of our personality.

If someones a screamer or a yeller, it's not going to get better during a crisis. It's only going to get worse.

And I think training yourself to do that and then soliciting feedback, I probably did not solicit feedback as much as I should have when I was younger. I think as I got older, I was much better at that. *Solicit feedback from your organization.* Am I doing what you need me to do during these situations? What can I do better? And then what am I doing that really helps if I need to reinforce?

#4 - WHAT ADVICE WOULD YOU GIVE SOMEONE WHO WANTS TO IMPROVE THEIR CRISIS LEADERSHIP?

What advice would I give someone who wants to improve their crisis leadership? I think that's a really interesting question. There's a lot of advice I could probably give myself, or I'm still seeking advice from others.

But from that perspective, from my perspective, what I would offer to others is to know your people and help them grow as leaders. Know what their strengths are. Know what their weaknesses are. If they will be called upon in a crisis situation to do something, you need to give them the opportunities to do that now. The first time cannot be when you're asking it of them.

And if you're going to ask them to do that in an exceptionally stressful environment, you've got to create ways to expose them to that. So, that can either be through training, or it could be through just general scenarios. It could be through reading, but you've got to help them prepare to be a crisis leader.

Again, you've also got to know your professions. You've got to know your job, and you've got to know the profession you're in. If it's fire, if it's EMS, if it's the corporate world, if it's military, whatever, you have to be an expert in your profession.

And you've got to know your roles and responsibilities. You've got to know your subordinates' roles and responsibilities.

There cannot be a knowledge gap during a crisis. You can't be hunting for the information you should have, or you should be familiar with during a crisis. That should be second nature. And again, that can be hard to find the time to do that, and arguably if you don't, then that can really lead to a larger crisis environment than what you need.

You have to train to be a good leader, and this gets into what I just talked about.   It just doesn't happen in even natural leaders or people who say they're natural leaders.

They've got to work at it.

They research it. They do self-assessments. They seek advice. They seek other opinions. They strive to improve. They read history. They read about leadership. They become a student of leadership in crisis situations and in business and in a variety of things, but it takes study.

One of the best ways, other than what I just mentioned to *study is to study others. Learn from others.*

There are good and bad examples of leadership and crisis leadership every single day. Be looking for it.

Think about it. Have a journal. *Use these experiences to help yourself grow and to assess yourself, because I guarantee you know what makes you.*

What you see in a leader during a crisis, you know what works, and you know what doesn't. So take advantage of those opportunities to then learn and adjust your leadership style.

#5 - WHO IS A CRISIS LEADER THAT INFLUENCED YOUR CAREER?

Who's a crisis leader that influenced my career. That one's a hard one for me to answer, and I'm not exactly sure how to answer it.

There were several, and they changed each time I moved up in the organization. The reason they changed is because I observed crisis decision-making from a different perspective.

As you move up into an organization, what worked for you or what impacted your leadership and the things that influenced your leadership and the things that you had to consider in those environments differ. The outcomes you are trying to achieve could honestly be different.

I would say that throughout my career, I probably had a half dozen individuals that really influenced my leadership skills regardless if it was in a crisis or not. My leadership skills. Each one of them gave me a very, very unique perspective based on that time and that environment. Again, it became cumulative over time, where I would build on myself. It did change as I moved up throughout the organization.

One of those half dozen or so I learned almost all of my negative traits on leadership, but I think you've got to look at those types of experiences as beneficial. While maybe painful during the time, they do shape you preferably for the better over time.

Don't have one individual, but I will say that I do have about a good half dozen or so that really influenced who I am and how I developed as a leader and continue to grow and develop as a leader. About three or four of them, I still use as mentors to continue that growth process. I hope that helps.

KEY TAKEAWAYS

- Trust and empower your people
- Set the example in all you do
- Solicit feedback on how you're doing
- Provide people the opportunity to fail before a crisis
- Use yourself as an example when you fail
- Help people be a crisis leader before they have to be a crisis leader
- Learn from both positive and negative leaders
- Journal your crisis successes and failures
- Provide resources, support, and direction
- Prevent knowledge gaps during a crisis
- Learn from positive and negative traits of other leaders
- Ask people for advice ... before there is a crisis
- Train to be a good leader, it doesn't happen naturally

MIKE MCKENNA – DISASTER RESPONSE/INVESTIGATIONS

Home	Dallas-Ft. Worth, Texas
Then	Disaster Responder & Private Investigator
Now	Leadership Consultant
Contact	**LinkedIn:** michaelmckenna1/
Quote	*"Zig when others zag ..."*

WHY MIKE IS A CRISIS LEADER

The journey to 'crisis leadership' is not the same for everyone.

For some, they learn to operate in a crisis-filled environment, then gradually develop leadership skills to lead others in that environment. Many fire and law enforcement crisis leaders come to mind.

For others, they gain leadership acumen over time, and then when a crisis occurs, they step into the moment to lead. Many business leaders come to mind.

For me, I suppose it's a little bit of both.

However, since I never started out to be a crisis leader, it's also a bit strange to refer to myself as one now.

So why am I included in this interview project? For starters, my wife encouraged me to participate. Besides being a good steward of her advice, she also suggested it might be hypocritical if I didn't. Fair point.

Because my background is non-traditional, my experiences have provided me with a much different perspective than most folks.

Sharing those experiences provides you, the reader, with a wider range of material to evaluate as you ponder your own crisis leadership.

#1 - WHAT IS A CRISIS LEADER?

What is a crisis leader?

A crisis leader is someone who is a leader of themselves, and then is a leader of others.

They lead with courage and competence and compassion, and they make sure they get to an acceptable conclusion of the crisis, whether it's big or small, even if it's messy along the way.

#2 - PLEASE SHARE AN EXAMPLE WHEN YOU RELIED ON YOUR CRISIS LEADERSHIP?

Two examples of crisis leadership of my own experience.

The first one dates, I guess in the 1990s, I managed a private investigative office.

I had a secretary; I had a staff of investigators. We were quite successful focusing on one area of business that involved the investigation of intellectual property rights, or counterfeiting diversion, cargo theft, that sort of thing, for a pretty impressive roster of international customers, clients, that made consumer products.

Most of the targets of our investigation were criminals, and some of them were organized criminals.

And so, we would work when we had enough evidence, we would work with our partners within local, state, and federal law enforcement, in order to facilitate a criminal takedown and seizure and arrest of the offenders.

Again, we were pretty successful, and working through one of our informants, we heard that one of the organized crime groups didn't find it very funny that we were making such a large impact on their illicit dealings.

They sent the word out that I, along with my staff and family, were to be killed.

It was not something that I had prepared really myself for, and it was pretty disruptive for all the obvious reasons. Initially, I really had no idea what to do and did not exhibit much of any leadership, even though my staff was looking to me for that very thing.

It took about a day for me to kind of gather my wits and just started moving in a forward direction. I rallied the group, and we decided we were going to modify our operations a little bit with the way we communicated and traveled and worked our other cases, that sort of thing.

I had to contend with running a business because we had other paying customers. We had bills to pay.

And of course, we had the extended families that were quite concerned that a job was going to lead to potential harm to ourselves from others.

So, it was quite a crisis during that time, and obviously, I spent some time networking with our partners in law enforcement to try to seek out the origin of that information to determine how viable of a threat it was to my staff and to me.

It was a trying time and what I discovered, it took about a week by the way for us to learn that the threat was a little bit overblown and while we were always vulnerable because of the work we did, there wasn't a real imminent threat to us being killed, which was a bit of a relief, but it really brought into focus the importance of crisis leadership.

And how I started not being a very strong crisis leader, but what I learned from that is that even though I didn't have a perfect plan, I took action.

I kept in mind what our priorities were, which is personal safety to those people that I was responsible for, and ultimately, we're able to look back on that as a stronger group, and obviously, nothing happened to me or any of my staff.

So that was a crisis leadership example where I started slow and ended a little bit stronger.

Another example would be in 2005, I was in New Orleans with my federal Urban Search and Rescue team, and we had responded to Hurricane Katrina, which was a hurricane that you probably know if you're seeing this in the modern era.

There was a tremendous amount of damage, it collapsed some levees, and it flooded the city of New Orleans, with 10 to 20 feet of water in many places.

Early on, we, meaning our group, our forward operations group, had found kind of a beachhead on the side of a highway. We were setting up to start to do some reconnaissance in the neighborhood, and we were met by a citizen, that we ended up calling Boudreaux. He had his boat, and he brought us a note that said, the note was from an apartment complex, and their manager saying they had some critically ill people and that they were out of power. They were underwater, help, help, help, that sort of thing.

My operations chief handed it to me and to my partner and to the state trooper and asked if Boudreaux could take us to that place so that we could size it up and determine what sort of response was necessary.

So the three of us got into Boudreaux's boat, so the four of us went an estimated two miles away from where we had put into the water.

Only Boudreaux knew where this was.

About a quarter-mile away and we hit some dry ground, where the boat couldn't pass, obviously.

So, the three of us: Myself, Brad, my partner, and the trooper, we waded through this water in order to get to this apartment complex where, sure enough, it was about eight stories high.

There were a lot of people milling around, and when they saw us show up in uniforms, they thought it was gonna be a good day.

I had noted an area that was a little bit elevated and dry that would serve as a viable LZ (helicopter landing zone), and when we went into the apartment complex, everyone wanted a ride home. So I tried to get ahold of my team on the radio. I was unsuccessful, so I went to the roof, which I think was around seven or eight floors high, and tried to reach our forward base by radio and was unsuccessful, we just hadn't set up a (long-range radio) network yet.

I did reach a passing helicopter, who told me that we needed to "take a number."

And about that same time, the trooper joined us and said that Boudreaux had taken off with the boat, and so now we were identical to everyone in the apartment complex.

We were stranded, and we were facing the same crisis everyone else was.

So at that point, my training and our training had always been focused on protecting ourselves, protecting our team, protecting our victim. And so I found that I mainly defaulted to that and felt like even though it was certainly an unpleasant situation, being in that environment without any support and without anyone knowing where we were, I did feel like our team that we were, at least in the short term, going to be okay.

And so after that, my focus really as a crisis leader was on putting the pieces together to come up with a solution. And that went to the welfare of the people in the apartment complex.

I encountered a surgeon who was in a kayak, paddling through the city, checking on folks, and I commandeered him and asked him if he would help perform some medical triage to determine who was the most critical.

There was another forward team from another USAR group that I contacted, or that they passed by the building, and so I contacted them and negotiated for them to divert from their mission in order to help us. They agreed to give my team and me a ride, and they agreed to give some of our evacuees a ride, the ones that were the most critical.

So, we eventually were able to make it out of there.

We were eventually able to help some people.

It was not an ideal circumstance, but in retrospect, as I have retold that story before, it came across as a much greater crisis to the people listening than it did to me. Simply because we *had a plan that was based on some core competencies, which is the importance of protecting ourselves, protecting our team, or protecting our victim.* And then every objective grows out of those requirements in order to get to the finish line even though it was quite messy.

It was an imperfect situation, but I was gratified that we were able to leave New Orleans better than we found it.

#3 - WHAT DO YOU KNOW NOW THAT YOU WISH YOU KNEW THEN?

A list of things that I know now that I wish I knew then is a pretty long and distinguished list.

There are a couple of them that do jump out.

In no particular order, one is *the importance of embracing the importance of a repeatable process.*

Automation is a very helpful tool, particularly for crisis leaders that can institute planning processes, procedures, decision making matrices, checklists, that sort of thing.

Delegate those, and it frees up that crisis leader to make some of the more strategic, weightier type decisions that we look to from those crisis leaders.

You don't have to know everything, and you don't have to be able to do everything either.

That is part and parcel of a Type A leader that wants to do everything and be everything. But they're not going to be very effective.

So I think early in our careers we try to do more than we probably should, whereas, when we *learn that the art of delegation and we learn the art of collaboration, and relationship building and networking, and we can reach out to others that have a skill set that maybe we don't in order to augment our leadership.*

Because remember *leadership is not about us, it's about the people that we're leading and reaching a positive outcome.* So, humility is an important aspect of that.

And the last one is, *you don't have to be in the lead to be a leader.*

And, this is something that has taken me a long time to learn personally because I don't come from a traditional military, fire, or police background. And while I've had some notable leadership and crisis leadership roles, there has always been a bit of an outsider feeling that I have simply because I don't come from some of those traditional backgrounds.

And so, as I've learned to overcome that it's allowed me to grow more as a leader.

And then the second part of that is that everyone should be a leader, and the *best leaders that I know are empowering because they generate confidence and courage and compassion among the people that are followers to turn them into leaders as well.*

And when that happens, I tell you 'Katy bar the door' there's really no stopping that particular response, organization, et cetera.

So wherever we are in the organization, whether we are on the outside looking in whether we are at the bottom looking up, *everybody can and frankly should develop, hone, and enhance our leadership skills.*

And I wish I knew that then as I know now.

#4 - WHAT ADVICE WOULD YOU GIVE SOMEONE WHO WANTS TO IMPROVE THEIR CRISIS LEADERSHIP?

The advice that I would give someone who wants to improve their crisis leadership is one of my favorite questions because it really strikes at the core of what this interview project has been about and that is to pay it forward to those people that are coming up from behind, or behind us.

Those that are wanting to, as my dad used to call it, "improve the breed." And there are some quality answers to this question, and I'm going to make an attempt to add to it if I can.

In no particular order, some of the advice that I would give is something that I pass along to my children, and I try to live my life this way, and that is, *don't be afraid to zig when everyone else is zagging.*

There's a lot of good that can come out of that. There are maybe some unpredicted challenges that can come out of that as well, but *real insight comes from looking at things from a different perspective.*

So there's a lot of information out there right now that you can find about the years and the history of a particular way of doing things, and while those are good foundation items, I really encourage future leaders to also *embrace maybe the non-traditional outlets for information* as well.

And don't be afraid to be a little bit innovative, because that's ultimately where you're going to make the greatest improvements.

Relationships, oh my gosh, those are so important.

There's a *mistaken belief that a lot of people have, unfortunately, that they must be the smartest person in the room.* If you encounter this person run, because not only are they not the smartest person in the room, their hubris and their lack of humility is going to sabotage whatever it is you're currently working on together.

Seriously, run away.

The solution to that is to build relationships and to understand that you are not the smartest person in the room, neither am I, neither is anyone else for this interview project. But you can build relationships, and when you find yourself in a predicament, you can tap into that network and those relationships for them to bring their strengths to bear in the absence of the strength that you have yourself.

Know that a crisis is messy.

And by understanding that you're dealing with a world of imperfection in a crisis, you're not just moving paper from one side of the desk to the other. *You're actually managing and navigating through a very messy crisis by its very nature is going to be imperfect, and when you understand it's imperfect you're less likely to get caught up in some of the minutiae, and you're more likely and more empowered, I think, to stay focused on the finish line which is where, ultimately, you're trying to reach safely and swiftly.*

The next one is going to be 'mindset' and *having a mindset that embraces maybe the worst possible scenario.*

A lot of people might say that that's the last thing you want to do but in my experience if you know that the worst thing that can happen is gonna be lots of death and destruction and you know what that looks like and smells like and tastes like then you can come up with some pretty good mitigations to navigate around that.

But if you deny yourself and deny others what that worst-case scenario will look like, then when it happens, or if it happens, it's gonna surprise you and everyone else, and that's not what we look for in a crisis leader.

So don't be afraid to *venture into the dark side to imagine what that worst-case scenario would look like because then you can come up with better plans to navigate around it.*

And the last piece of advice that I would give, frankly, is to make sure that you are signed up for one or more of the newsletters at **TEAM-Solutions.US**.

That's my website, and I relentlessly share and create content focused solely on your improvement as a crisis leader.

That's it.

#5 - WHO IS A CRISIS LEADER THAT INFLUENCED YOUR CAREER?

Who is a crisis leader that has influenced my career is probably the most unfair question. Simply because I got to pick the interview subjects for this project and every single one of them is a tremendous influence on me. For all the obvious reasons as you read and hear their stories.

I learned something from all of them.

I have had the opportunity to serve directly for some of them in this interview project, and so I have seen their crisis leadership first-hand, which is again why one of the reasons why I selected them.

And some of the others, I have just been around them enough to really get a good sense as to the caliber of crisis leaders that they are or were in their active career.

The next category of influential crisis leaders to me, and I have a couple of them, are all the willfully lousy leaders I've had in my life so far. Willful because they knew a better way and didn't take it, at the cost of everyone that served under them. They each illustrate an important lesson about leaders in that *if they are not still growing too, they are not worth following for very long.*

We all take it on the chin occasionally from having bad managers and bad leaders; I certainly am not an exception.

And I've learned the difference between leadership and management, and I've also learned that bad leaders still can teach us something while we're actively trying to get away from them.

Because I try myself to have a growth mindset, and I'm attracted to those leaders that also are trying to continue to develop even after they've left their primary leadership role.

And so I'm always *primed, therefore, to look for, listen for, and detect the presence of good leadership, wherever it may be.*

Whether it's a child, whether it's a young adult, whether it's an aged adult, or even whether it's an organization that's run by people.

So the next leader that's out there, the next person or the person that I haven't met influences me because I'm always looking for them, to learn from them.

And then the last influential crisis leader, frankly, is you.

Because as this project has developed, I'm inspired by the thought of being able to pass along some of these stories, some of these lessons to help you who is likely a new or emerging, or even experienced crisis leader that's just trying to be even better.

You're the reason that this project exists, and so you are probably the greatest influential leader solely because you're the one that's going to be running the world after the rest of us are gone. *Thank you.*

KEY TAKEAWAYS

- Take action, even when you're in unfamiliar territory
- Be prepared to zig when others are zagging
- Listen to your spouse's advice
- Learn from everyone, including lousy leaders
- Serve others, always
- Keep your radar on for examples of good leadership
- Rely on your training as a foundation of decision-making
- Grow or be left out
- Gain insight by changing perspectives
- Build relationships in and outside of your normal circle
- Maintain a network of other leaders
- Embrace non-traditional outlets for information
- Accept imperfection to reach an acceptable result
- Acknowledge the worst so you can plan for the best
- Consume educational content relentlessly
- Develop and engage with repeatable processes
- Be a leader regardless of where you are in the hierarchy
- Avoid the belief that you must do everything yourself
- Develop priorities, then build objectives and strategies to achieve them

RORY REHBECK - CAPT.; LOS ANGELES CO. FIRE DEPT

Home	Grand Junction, Colorado
Then	Fire Captain; Los Angeles County Fire Dept
Now	Independent Public Safety Professional
Contact	**LinkedIn:** rory-rehbeck-34691917/
Quote	*"Trust your people to do what you've trained them to do ..."*

WHY RORY IS A CRISIS LEADER

Rory was one of my earliest mentors when I became involved in Urban Search and Rescue (USAR). He helped shape my understanding of disasters and how to respond to them effectively.

As the former chairperson of FEMA's prestigious Search Working Group Rory led many of the advances in search and rescue that helped fuel our future successes. His fingerprints are on almost every successful federal search and rescue policy and procedure used today.

Although quiet and humble, Rory has held a leadership role in nearly every federal disaster in the United States in the last 25 years.

As for leadership during a crisis, he's definitely *'been there and done that.'*

Rory is a trusted ally and a dear friend, and it's an honor to capture his story.

#1 - WHAT IS A CRISIS LEADER?

That's a good question, Mike.

As Emergency Responders, if you look in the public's eye, everything is a crisis to the general public.

And you never know when the situation is gonna, what you think is a simple situation is gonna turn, and present a different situation when you arrive or in the middle of it. So you have to be flexible to manage that incident because how that incident starts is going to dictate how that incident continues.

If it starts bad, it's not managed well; the incident can turn really bad.

But if it's managed well, it will have a better outcome. Both for the team and also for our customers. And it doesn't matter how big the crisis is.

I don't look, for me, *I never looked at the size of the crisis; I always looked at what was being presented to me and trying to manage that.*

That particular response or incident, whether it be somebody with a broken leg, or a major incident where you're doing large search operation, or a large brush fire.

#2 - PLEASE SHARE AN EXAMPLE WHEN YOU RELIED ON YOUR CRISIS LEADERSHIP?

Boy, looking back, I'm looking back 33 years of response to incidents.

Taking a large incident, we managed in Houston after Hurricane Ike, we helped manage search operations, and *getting everybody on the same page as far as terminology and operations.*

And I thought it was a big step forward after Katrina.

And the process that we worked on during that, prior to that time, with search marking, search definitions, and then the process, the tactical process.

But seeing that all come together and making sure everybody was on the same page, to me, that was one of the, to me, a milestone for search operations in large area or wide area searches.

And so being in the leadership role of that and seeing it come to fruition, I thought was pretty substantial.

And that it has really paved the way for future operations that have occured over the past ten years.

#3 - WHAT DO YOU KNOW NOW THAT YOU WISH YOU KNEW THEN?

Okay, what you know now that you wish you knew then.

Oh boy, I think probably, probably my early years in the fire service. I wish there would have been more training and leadership offered throughout the department.

Our department, for a large department, had a very small training staff. And it was hard to find those leadership type classes.

Of course, after the years you kinda pick up on things, and you're around different leaders, and you learn their leadership style.

I wish I would have known that when I was younger. It comes back to trusting your people.

The training that you do and trusting your people to do what you've trained them to do.

I think for me that, I mean, we did our training, and the one thing I always do is I trusted my people to do what they were trained to do.

But on another portion of that is the additional leadership training.

Now from what I understand, the department I was with, which was Los Angeles County Fire Department, they're doing more leadership training.

That's a good thing.

#4 - WHAT ADVICE WOULD YOU GIVE SOMEONE WHO WANTS TO IMPROVE THEIR CRISIS LEADERSHIP?

What advice would you give someone who wants to prove their crisis leadership?

In the past, of course, after I retired, I read some books about leadership that were written by some retired military. And their process of how they established their mission objectives and how they proceed in doing a mission. And I think those books are out there and, as a leader I think you need to look at those and read 'em.

And if you see any courses, or just a one day class on leadership for emergency responders, or even just a general leadership class. I think it would be, behoove someone who was coming up to take that or those particular classes.

And if you see somebody that you admire or you've worked with, and you like their leadership style, start asking questions. Go to them and ask them.

It is basically interviewing them to find out their leadership style and where they want to learn from it.

I know we have a number of people that are as emergency responders who have been in the military. The military offers a lot of leadership courses. Those people would obviously have those leadership courses, but for the general public, get out there, and you're gonna have to beat the bushes a little bit, but those courses are out there.

#5 - WHO IS A CRISIS LEADER THAT INFLUENCED YOUR CAREER?

Who's a crisis leader that influenced your career?

I was a captain at a battalion headquarters, and I worked for a battalion chief.

One of my first fires with him is, he says you got this kid, I'm here to support you, but handle it. And I'm going, oh boy.

And there were a lot of things that he did like that. And basically, he was mentoring me by doing that, and to promote.

I never promoted above captain, but he was great in doing that by, if you get to a point where you can't handle it, let me know, elsewise, handle it.

And I always appreciated that.

It really kind of led me, and basically, he's saying, yes, I trust you on handling it, and I trust my people.

That was to me, that was always a big influence in trusting my people in doing their jobs. I always appreciated Bob for doing that.

KEY TAKEAWAYS

o Learn from other leaders, including the military
o Start well to finish well
o Seek out and enroll in leadership training courses
o Focus on what's known about the crisis, not how big it is
o Trust your people to do what they're trained to do

TIM HARRISON – DIR. AT

OUTREACH FOR ANIMALS

Home	Dayton, Ohio
Then	Public Safety Officer
Now	Director at Outreach for Animals
Contact	Outreachforanimals.org
Quote	*"Trust your professional instinct ..."*

WHY TIM IS A CRISIS LEADER

I first met Tim while working as part of an instructor cadre teaching current and future incident managers.

His magnetic personality draws people in, and his depth of knowledge on almost any topic makes it hard to turn away.

From a background consisting of mixed martial arts to emergency response to exotic animal rescue, Tim is one of the most interesting men I know.

It's an honor to be able to share his crisis leadership stories; many` ripped from the headlines.'

As you'll see, his diverse background plays a huge part in his diverse set of skills he uses to lead himself and others during a crisis.

Be sure to learn more about his latest and arguably one of the most important projects he's involved with: his leadership of Outreach For Animals, the #1 advocate for proper behavior around animals.

#1 - WHAT IS A CRISIS LEADER?

A crisis leader, to me, is somebody that ... It's like a quarterback of a football team.

I was a quarterback, and when the huddle gets around you before you go into the stressful, you know, play that you're gonna be having there in the football field with everybody watching, the huddle around you, they're all looking at you for confidence.

They're looking at you for trust.

They're looking to you for communication, what we need to do as a team together.

And to me, it's like being a good quarterback.

So when you do get into a crisis later, *there has to be somebody that everybody looks to, trusts, and is also able to understand the communications.*

They look at ya and say, "You're giving me what I need to do to accomplish my task, what my objective is."

So to me, it's like being a quarterback.

But I'd also throw in, too, since I'm in the fight game, it's like being a good cornerman also, too, because your team's out there working for ya, and you're going to have to know their strengths, their weaknesses, of the team members.

So when they come to you, and you give them a job or something to do that they can't do, and they're not gonna be able to accomplish that job, it's gonna break the team down all the way through.

So you don't-- You have to know your team members, you have to be able to look at them as a good cornerman, put that Vaseline on their eyes and their nose, and send them back into the fight, knowing that they could continue to fight and continue doing what you need 'em to do, to hopefully win that fight.

So to me, a good crisis leader is somebody that's a quarterback of a football team, then when you get in that huddle, before we get into it, they all look at you, they're waiting for your communications, they're waiting for you to tell 'em what's gonna happen, and they're trusting you.

And make sure that play runs well.

And also being a bit of a cornerman. Just be there for 'em, you know, when things go bad, go good, you're standing there, you're ready for 'em. "Come to me, and we're gonna work this out."

#2 - PLEASE SHARE AN EXAMPLE WHEN YOU RELIED ON YOUR CRISIS LEADERSHIP?

There have been many situations, being a public safety officer- I'm a police officer, firefighter, paramedic, all wrapped into one.

But I've got to trust my own crisis leadership, management skills, and also as a crew commander, but I've had some unusual situations too, that most officers and most government officials will not run into on a regular basis and I want to bring that out.

So that when it does happen, it doesn't stymie people.

People get a real *baptism in reality* when they have two African lions running loose on the interstate, and they have no idea how- they just freeze.

People freeze, even if you're a master at critical thinking, you still freeze because that is a bizarre, abstract situation happening.

I've had that situation happen with two African lions running on the interstate of Ohio attacking cars.

We were able to put up a perimeter, and I calmed the situation down, I had the skills and the experience to be able to tell people these lions were only going to stay with a certain area. They're not going to cross the river. They're not going to do these things that people are worried about, and we were able to calm the situation down.

Then I had the Superbowl of that kind of situation happen, was the Zanesville massacre in Zanesville, Ohio in 2011 where a gentleman that I had had confrontations with over the years, Terry Thompson, turned 56 of the most dangerous animals in the world loose on the city of Zanesville.

We had 38 big cats- that's tigers, lions, leopards, cougars. Then we had grizzly bears, black bears, uh, wolves, primates running loose- some primates have herpes B virus, which some of the officers wanted to shoot, and I had to calm everybody down and say, Whoa whoa, we can't shoot that animal because it's infected.

If you shoot it and it doesn't kill it right away, it's going to run with that infection through the community.

So in that kind of situation, being involved with a critical thinking situation like that and being sit down as looked at in the incident command post as somebody that- "can you help us? Can you come in here and help set this situation up?"

I was able to step in and tell them, "This is what we need to do. We do need to shoot the animals." Because it was getting dark, we can't dart these animals.

These are questions that were being brought up by the media and everyone else.

So, that situation in Zanesville was a really big wake up call across the world for our law enforcement and firefighters to be able to handle these kinds of situations because more of this is going to happen down the road, but I also learned with my critical uh, thinking and my critical leadership uh, abilities I was able to step in and calm the situation down.

Things were out of control, and everybody was giving advice. Everybody was an expert- government officials were experts, of course, right.

I had to step in and say, "Listen guys, let me show you the easy way to do this. Let's sit down- just like the quarterback of the team- let's sit down, guys and huddle up here in the instant command post, and make a decision of what we're going to do.

Stick with that decision, and I'll be the voice of what happens- I'll be the one to step up and say, "I was the critical leader in this one. We made the decision.

Sheriff Lutz was actually the incident commander, but he did exactly what he was supposed to do. So we were able to handle a situation that was totally out of control, unbelievable, could not even be- I couldn't ever dream of it, in my lifetime, and it was a situation that has been repeated on smaller scales, as we've learned now.

The tiger was loose in Georgia, on interstate 75, actually was going down towards children getting ready to get on a bus. This just happened this year, and the officers were making quick decisions and it- they needed to step up and just make the decision: we have to kill it.

When you make the decision, for public safety on what your decision is, you have to stick with it, and that's what I would say is my uh, Superbowl of uh, critical leader.

Working in that kind of capacity because that was, to a point, where I have never done this before, that large of a scale, nobody has.

And it's like ... People are used to earthquakes. We can do that. We can do a tornado. We can do all these incidents. Okay, 38 big cats. Grizzly bears, 56 altogether- C'mon. Loose in the community, and people were calling in 911 continually. "I got a lion in my backyard." "I got a tiger running down the interstate." "I got a bear going after one of my dogs."

It was one of those situations, it was very abstract, and we were able to handle that situation and keep it within a perimeter, and I was very proud of that.

#3 - WHAT DO YOU KNOW NOW THAT YOU WISH YOU KNEW THEN?

You know, what I know now, and I wish I knew then.

One thing is that I wish I would have stuck with my instincts more because back then, *I was going by book knowledge, tabletop stuff a lot, which is great, which is great, but I think a lot of times we lose our instinct, our natural instinct, to do what's right.*

I know most people's natural instinct is to run away from a disaster, to run. Our instinct is to go into a disaster.

We're made differently. We're wired differently as first responders, so we go with that instinct but also go with the instinct of survival, and to pay attention to your pack, let's just say like a wolf pack.

We're going in.

Use that instinct to look for your people, care for your people. Don't get tunnel vision.

Look at the situation like you would look at it as maybe even as a primitive individual going into a hut.

We're going to go in and look at the whole situation. We forgot that.

We've been civilized a little bit too much to the point where we'll hesitate sometimes when we should go ahead and take that natural instinct, that first thought that's in our minds, what we have.

Back then, I hesitated a lot, and I wish. There are some situations I think I could have handled a lot better if I just went with my natural instinct just to go, and we call it professional instinct now. I have a lot of guys out here I work with.

It's called a professional instinct because you say natural instinct, people are like, "Oh, you're like an animal, right?"

No, *professional instinct, and we all have it.*

I learned a lot of that as time went on by working with surgeons when I worked in surgery, where I saw them do some amazing stuff that wasn't by the book, and I'm thinking, "Where did this come from?" And they would tell you, "Instinct, brother. Instinct. That's why they call it medical arts."

And I'm thinking, "Let's bring that to the disaster world."

So, if you're standing there, and you're thinking, "I need three engines over here," and all of a sudden, your natural instinct says, "You know, I could do this and save my people a lot of work and protect them better. Let's go with that."

It may go against what the book says, but sometimes it's gonna maybe save lives and be a quicker, safer way to do it, and I wish I had the confidence I have now because back then, confidence was something you earn.

I've watched that with a lot of people. You earn it.

It's one of those things where there are cocky people. Stay away from them.

Like I always say, "If somebody's an expert, somebody's gonna get hurt. Look out."

And it happens in all fields, but confidence-wise, I wish I was a little bit more confident.

I'd have stepped up when the chief was asking questions and said, "Chief, I got a feeling here, from my years of experience, working here, that we need to get this guy moved from here to here, and it might be an easier way to do it." Now, I know a lot of young guys feel that way, too.

When you're in the situation, having a pow-wow, and you just don't feel like I can't say anything.

I think *confidence is not being overly confident, not being narcissistic, but just saying you've got something and that's where a good critical leader comes in to be able to listen, to listen to what's going on, and look at his team* and go, "Bob, what do you think? Are we all on the same page? Tell me what you feel," and they should have that three or four times before that at the bar six weeks ago, or the restaurant you guys all ate at, or the training session you had six months ago.

That should have broken ice back then. That should have been a situation where you don't keep your mouth shut.

You tell me. If you don't tell me, I'm gonna be mad, so it's already there before the incident occurs, so you already have that groundwork already laid out, and I learned that, and it's really sad.

Not from the emergency world that I got involved with, but working in the hospital world because you would think these surgeons were overly confident and cocky.

They're confident, but they'll look at you, and they're looking at the nurses, and if you've ever been in the emergency room, which I know a lot of people have, look at the doctors ask the emergency room nurses, "What do you think? What's going on?"

You'll see that, and there's teamwork there, a trust, and that's one thing I wish I would have stepped up and said a few things because I saw things that happened that could have probably had a better outcome for everyone involved.

#4 - WHAT ADVICE WOULD YOU GIVE SOMEONE WHO WANTS TO IMPROVE THEIR CRISIS LEADERSHIP?

One thing, if you want to improve your crisis leadership, I've learned over the years is to be more involved with what's going on.

Read a lot, watch a lot of videos and training. Take what you need out of it.

I'm kind of like an old Bruce Lee martial artist, where you look at all the different skills and all the things that are out there people have done, speak with the people that have been through the situation, have been through those fights.

Learn what worked for them and what didn't work for them.

Write it down; keep it in a log. Put it somewhere so that when you get into that situation, it's not going to be a surprise. "Oh, I know what this gentleman did, a friend of mine did, on an earthquake. This is what happened, this is what he did wrong, this is what he did right."

So gather as much information as you can, learn as much as you can, go to as much training as you can, which is good, take what you need out of it.

It's one of those situations where people gather too much, and they have too much in their heads.

I always liked that Far Side comic, where the little kid raises his hand in class and says, "May I be excused? My brain's full."

You don't want to have too full a brain. You want to have bullet points. You want to have things that are going to hit. Boom, boom, boom, boom, when it gets into that fight.

It's the same as a kickboxer, the same as a mix martial artist.

You get out there; you're not gonna have a whole bunch of stuff, you're gonna keep the techniques that work for you and keep them valuable and try to work them into what other people have done, and not successfully.

But what they have done successfully, I'm going to use that technique. And that's what I've learned over the years.

The one thing is, too, is to try to understand that, if somebody tells you something, they're not trying to be obnoxious. I've had a lot of times over the years, I've actually shut people off, "this guy is trying to tell me something, you know, blah, blah, blah." No, listen to everyone, listen, listen, listen, listen.

It's both very important that you listen and pay attention and absorb everything you can.

And if you don't listen, that's when you become a person that becomes stagnant, and you're a danger in the crisis leadership world.

If you stagnate, and we all know those people, "that's the way we've always done it," no.

You gotta make sure that you look at the situation, all situations, and be able to adapt and learn from it.

And as we said earlier, make sure before anything happens, before you get into the situation, y'all know each other. Your team knows each other, you know the neighboring city, you know the people that you work with, so when it comes together, you're not gonna be in one of those scams where I don't know what you do.

So the main thing is, listen, work and learn from each other, know each other, that's the biggest thrill, is to get everybody to know each other and your surrounding area and go to as many national trainings as you can to learn from everybody from around the country.

Most of the time you're going to learn it's not going to be in the classroom, it's going to be at the restaurant that night or the bar.

That's where you're gonna learn cause they're gonna tell you the truth. And that's where you're gonna learn your most stuff.

Also, too, learn things like ... I was teaching them at the Zanesville massacre. One of the things I taught is don't say "This is the way you do it." You come in gently and say, "Hey, by the way, let me give you a little advice. Let me throw this out on the table." That's how you do it.

You don't run in there, puff up your chest, and act like your the king. You walk in and say, listen, listen, listen. Herpes B, you've got a veterinarian standing right here. Herpes B, you can't shoot this animal. That's a moving hazardous material.

And that's what I would consider all dangerous exotics if anybody runs into them because they don't get vaccinations, they're a zoonotic nightmare.

You don't know what they have or where they've been. So with the situation with the Herpes B, with the primates, please, treat them as hazardous material.

And that way it clicks in your head, that's one of those bullet points we just talked about. It's already in your head, I can hit you, Mike, I can say, "Hey Mike, you might not be listening to me right now, but think about this for a second, hazardous material, hazardous material." Oh crap, that is right, that is a hazardous material.

You know, click to the responders that it'll put it in a category that they understand.

And it works.

If I walked up there and somebody from PETA, or one of these organizations and try to tell them, "Don't shoot the monkey, don't shoot the monkey." And somebody tried to say, "Oh, because you know, it carries disease." And that, I believe, myself and the majority of us would turn our brain off and not listen to it.

But if I approach you as a crisis leader and come up and say, "We got a hazardous material problem, here." "What?" that clicks, "What do you mean?" "Let me show you." Boom, boom, boom from that point, and then they understand it, "Oh crap, yeah, that is."

Shoot that monkey, he's running through the city, blood everywhere if we don't kill him right there on the spot.

So it's one of those situations where, *connections, you listen, you step in when you can, and you don't force your way in.*

That's some of the hints I give people and some of the things that would help you out. It helped me out over the, you know, 62 years old, it's helped me out over all these years, and I've learned some valuable skills from everybody I've worked with.

I've learned something from everybody I work with. And if you haven't, you're not listening.

#5 - WHO IS A CRISIS LEADER THAT INFLUENCED YOUR CAREER?

You know, I look back over my life, I had a lot of great, they weren't called crisis leaders back in the '70s, but I had a lot of great people that I dealt with over my life, and it's hard to pick a few, but one of the ones that sticks out the most was I worked at Piqua Medical Center.

I worked in surgery, and I would help the doctors. kind of a physician's assistant, kind of situation.

And I had a doctor, by the name of Dr. John Beachler. He was the oldest guy there, and it was a situation where I learned so much from him.

We had one night, we had a car accident with five cars involved, ten people, trauma, blood everywhere, and they're bringin' 'em to our hospital first to make the judgment.

We didn't really get into flying helicopters back then as much. It was one of those things where it was very, very stressful. Extremely stressful situation, for families screaming, people, kids, everything.

I watched him walk into the emergency room, and he called me in. I got in; I had the beeper. I got there. I watched him walk into the emergency room. There were two young doctors already there, and they were freakin' out. The nurses were freakin' out. I'm freakin' out, and you just don't know where to go.

The triage is like, yeah, I'll go ahead and start triaging. Where? Come on; we've got a kid over here. It's just like what?

You just gotta take that deep breath.

He walked in there, and you gotta remember I was just in my early 20s. He walks into that emergency room, and the first thing he goes, "Okay, honey." Called everybody honey. "Honey, let's see what we got here.

"Everybody relax. "Everything's gon' be fine."

And he walked into this woman screaming over her child. And he grabs her and touches on her back and says, "It's gon' be okay, honey." Everything's got that southern accent. "It's gon' be fine. "So won't you just step on outta here "and let me save your son's life."

And she just walked right out. And I'm thinkin', holy crap!

You know, this is like God just walked in here And everybody just, the nurses went I went oh, whoof, right.

And I watched him walk from patient to patient with me, "Tim, do this. "Tim, do that. "Come over here, do this. "MaryAnne do this. "Nurse do this, do this."

And it's like he was wading through this. It was like imagining as a firefighter, a house fully engulfed, and you had people like him. He's just wading through. You get that one. You get this one. Same exact thing.

We got everything under control within about I'm gonna throw out less than 25 minutes.

It was under control with him. And people were goin' to surgery. We had one guy stabilized. We did take him to Miami Valley Hospital.

It was like, it's just experience, but it was the way he was a stress and a crisis leader, which wasn't even a title back then.

He knew how to step into the mess with his confidence. He listened to everybody. Mama. He listened to the patients. He listened to every one of them. And everything's gonna be fine, honey.

And I know it's just his body rhythm, and the way he was and the confidence he had, that he was gonna take control of the situation.

And he knew us, what we could do. He didn't ask me to do anything I couldn't do. He knew what I could do, and he wanted me to do these things. And he asked the nurses. He sent 'em right over to do what they specialized in.

That's what I learned too. You want to fit the people, not in a situation where they're not, that's not their best qualities, let's say. MaryAnne, great IVs. "Well, okay, MaryAnne, honey, can you get over here "and get an IV in this little boy. "I see they're havin' a little trouble." She runs over and does it.

And it was one of those situations, where he knew the strengths, and then everything started clicking, 'cause everybody, oh, that's what I do! Okay, whoop, puts me back in the lane. And sometimes you need, as we used to teasingly call, when he comes in, it's like a sweet, kind, loving slap in the face. It's like stop! Oh, okay, go to work, right.

You know what you can do. And then, later on, we'd have like little critiques.

I didn't know what a critique was. But we'd always sit around, and then, "Okay, honey." He'd sit there and go, "This is what we did well." And he goes, "I didn't like this. "We'll just change it next time. "But everybody did a great job. "Love you all.", and he'd leave. But we had to sit there and go through what everybody did, what they did well. Some things he'd like to see differently. He'd just like to see it done differently. And then off he went.

So that was the guy that I learned that when the crap hits the fan, take a deep breath. I think in my mind, okay, honey. I don't say it. Everything's under control, that southern "okay, honey."

The other one was Sheriff Lutz, with the Zanesville Massacre. I've never seen an officer or a sheriff listen as much as he did, take it all in.

This was a crisis situation with no kind of rules before in the past, nothing to follow, no kind of idea even how to get your arms even slowly around this. And he sat, and he listens, he listens, he listens. And he listened to the guy that lived there, who was drunk. But he was trying to get information from him. He listened to everybody. And then he made a decision about what he was going to do. Made out what the deal was going to be.

But he listened to everybody.

And when he got through with it, he was worried that these organizations are gonna come and pickets and do all this stuff, like PETA and Humane Society and everything else, and I said, I'll take care of that for you. And I got ahead of it, and I got in contact with them, told them what went on. It's not the sheriff's fault. It's not the officer's fault, it's public safety, it's raining, and we all got in our 'lanes,' like I call it. Everybody gets in their lane.

Sheriff Lutz didn't talk about tigers. He didn't know anything about tigers, and I told him to stay away from that. You don't know anything about tigers. All you know is public safety, and that's your lane. Tim, you're the animal guy. That's you're lane, right now, not cops, not firemen. Your lane was dangerous animals, okay. So when I went to the media, when I spoke to the media, and I spoke to the organizations that they worried about, I gave them the heads up. Listen, guys, this is what happened, and they trusted me because they knew that's my expertise.

So these organizations that you would think would just bomb that place, which they were thinkin' about doin', stepped back, and go, I told 'em it wasn't them. It wasn't him. It was the laws that weren't passed. Go to where the bad guys are. If we had the laws, those animals wouldn't be there. It's not the sheriff's fault. And that's how we worked.

So to me, two of probably the greatest crisis leaders that I've met over my lifetime out of hundreds, literally hundreds, is Dr. John Beachler, and then-Sheriff Lutz from Zanesville, Ohio, in that county there.

And it was amazing to watch somebody that could have easily exploded or imploded, and that could have been Sheriff Lutz, and he didn't. He sat up when he knew what he had to do. We had to control this situation. Let's work it out, let's get it done.

And I'm tellin' you, Mike, it was overwhelming, the media. Nobody has any, you've seen disasters. We've all seen that on TV, shootings at bars. They had probably three times as much media there from all over the world than they did at probably the last bar shooting. They had satellites. They came in so quickly. We had TV Tokyo. We had everybody there.

And it was one of those situations, where I just went from one to the other and calmed it. And that's what, I think those crisis leaders showing me their style and how they do it, is almost like goin' to college and learning from the world's best, and I did.

And I would say, to me hanging around the guys and girls that have that quality, don't try to imitate them, just learn from it.

KEY TAKEAWAYS

o   Build and trust your professional instinct

o   Pay attention and absorb everything you can

o   Learn something from everyone your work with

o   Read a lot, watch a lot of videos and training

o   Stay away from cocky people

- Trust your skills so you can respond to the unexpected a/k/a 'baptism in reality'
- Learn from everybody but don't imitate them
- Stay within your area of knowledge

TODD YOUNG - CORPORATE LOSS PREVENTION DIR.

Home	Bellevue, Washington
Then	Corporate Loss Prevention Director - Coinstar, Inc.
Now	Consulting Director – Intl. Financial Management Advisory Company
Contact	**LinkedIn:** todd-young-seattle/
Quote	*"Common sense is a skillset ..."*

WHY TODD IS A CRISIS LEADER

Todd is an experienced and articulate leader with a well-developed skill for second-level thinking.

For example: When someone steps on the brakes of their car, they usually only think about their car coming to a stop. Todd instantly also anticipates the 2nd and 3rd order effects of that. Such as the guy driving two cars back will spill his coffee, and the bus three cars back will get stuck at the intersection.

A simple example, but most people, including many leaders, fail to see past the immediate impact in order to consider and evaluate the nuances and impacts that await around the next corner.

In his career so far, as a private-sector crisis leader, Todd's faced down more than a few first and second level calamities for his clients/employers.

As you'll see, his upbringing and personal pursuits all play a part in his approach to leadership.

Todd's insights have enabled him to lead himself and others in virtually every organization he's worked with … in calm and in risky conditions.

#1 - WHAT IS A CRISIS LEADER?

So what is a crisis leader?

I think it's an individual who remains calm under pressure, who can instill confidence in those with whom he's interfacing and leading.

It's a person who recognizes talent beyond their own capability and doesn't let their own hubris get in the way of success. In other words, they're not trying to be a hero. They're trying to instill an opportunity for a heroic outcome. [laughing]

So they're interested in results without getting credit. I always like to say that I want to take the blame, and I never want to take the credit.

I want the people that do the work to take the credit and get the credit. I really hate attention. I operate best under the cover of darkness.

So, and I also think, and we talked about this earlier, that *common sense being a skill set that is less common as the years go by.*

There's a poster that I love that says, *"Common sense, it's so goddamned rare "it's a superpower." And I truly believe that to be true.*

And the older I get, the truer it seems to be.

So I guess those are some of the characteristics I see in being a good crisis leader.

#2 - PLEASE SHARE AN EXAMPLE WHEN YOU RELIED ON YOUR CRISIS LEADERSHIP?

So this is a more difficult question, but I think of one scenario in my life as a kind of an enterprise risk manager working as an employee of a company that had a very serious problem with some failures in technology.

This is a company that operated coin exchange kiosks around the country. And when I was brought on, they were experiencing very high rates of loss nationally that historically had been attributed to internal theft thinking that they had transport employees that were stealing from them.

And to the extent that they were sending investigators out, spending lots of money on time and travel, meals, and interviewing employees that were associated with locations that are experiencing high volumes of loss.

In some cases, employees were confessing to just totally de minimis loss amounts. Yeah, I took 20 bucks, loose change that fell on the transport truck, and gave it to my kids so they could buy bubble gum. They would get confessions like that and spending thousands of dollars to do an investigation to get a $50 admission.

So I started looking at this from a technical technology perspective and saying, this is a machine and machines can fail.

One of my favorite stories growing up is the story of the Christmas ham. Have you heard of that?

The Christmas ham story goes like this:

> Mom's making the Christmas ham. Mom's making Christmas ham, and little Janie comes into the kitchen and sees that Ma has brought out a hacksaw and it's carving the end bone off the ham before she puts it in the oven.
>
> Little Janie says, "Mom, why are you carving the bone off the ham?" And she says, "Well, that's because what my mom, your grandma used to always do every year at Christmas. So that's what I do.
>
> So let's go ask her why she did it." So they go find grandma in the dining room sitting at the table, chatting. "Grandma, how come you used to cut the bone off for Christmas ham every year?" And she says, "Well, that's because my mom, your great-grandma used to always do that. So I did it.".
>
> So they go in to see great-grandma who's 95 years old and passed out with a scotch in the rocker in the living room by the fireplace. They wake her up and say,

"Great-grandma, why did you cut the end bone off the Christmas ham every year?" "Well, we homesteading there in Oklahoma, and all we had was this wood burning stove, and the ham wouldn't fit. So I had to send Johnny out to the barn and get the saw to carve that bone off so I could fit it in the stove."

So the moral of the story is you need to *ask why in order to figure out what's really going on.*

And my grandfather was a big influence on me.

He used to say, *"You need to ask why five times, and you'll get to the truth."*

So I started asking myself and asking people about why is it that we're losing money in these machines and is there a mechanical reason why that could be happening?

So one day, the lead technician for the company happened to be in the office. He was the guy that trained people all over the country, and he happened to be in town, and I went up to him and I said, "Is there a component on this machine that could break and if it broke would cause the machine to count the coin but not collect it, in other words, reject it and send it back to the customer?" He said, "Sure. There is...".

There is a device called a solenoid in the kiosk that sat behind the sensor that measured whether or not a coin was legitimate. And if that sensor identified a coin as being good, it would trigger the solenoid to shoot the coin into the acceptance barrel. But if that solenoid failed when the sensor told it to kick, the coin would be returned to the customer.

So if this solenoid failed, the coins that were counted as good coin by the sensor would be returned to the customer. The machine would pay off like a slot machine effectively over time as the solenoid would progressively fail further and further.

So with that one question of trying to ask why could this be happening, the guy answered a mystery that saved the company almost a million dollars a year in the years to come.

Because I took that information and implemented a program to monitor for every kiosk in the network, failures associated with certain denominations of coin that we could monitor progressively reduced the number of shortages associated with every denomination in every bin that was counted.

And we got to the point where we could predict that that solenoid was about to fail in a kiosk and replace it. *So we replaced a loss prevention problem with a preventative* *maintenance solution and saved the company $1 million a year.*

#3 - WHAT DO YOU KNOW NOW THAT YOU WISH YOU KNEW THEN?

I would say one of the lessons in life for me, and it's not restricted to crisis management, is really around the *importance of sticking to something*, maybe even beyond the point of a certain level of tolerance that you think you've just surpassed, and you can't take it anymore.

But I've had several occasions in my career where I made choices to move, where if I had not moved, I would've been a lot better off.

So one of the lessons in my mind is to really *have the discipline and the foresight and maybe even take the time to reach out to folks that might be able to provide you other perspectives* as you're making really important decisions around long-term, not just incidental or in-the-moment crisis situations, but very long-term situations that could affect your life, your family, your professional situation.

And really take the time to be very introspective as well as looking externally towards what the implications might be of making a decision.

The bottom line is I've made decisions that probably cost me millions of dollars because I left an opportunity just as it was coming to fruition.

And I have done that twice in my career. And on one of those occasions, I went just because the new opportunities sounded really fun, and I wasn't mature enough at the time to think about this may be a really fun thing to do, but is it the smartest thing to do from a long-term perspective?

So that's, I got to say definitely in retrospect, that's something I wish I knew now, or then that I know now.

#4 - WHAT ADVICE WOULD YOU GIVE SOMEONE WHO WANTS TO IMPROVE THEIR CRISIS LEADERSHIP?

I don't think there's any shortcut here in terms of improving leadership skills of any type, whether it's a crisis or otherwise.

It's a long and progressive series of learning events.

I think you have to be an intense reader and understand that, you know, *lessons from the past almost invariably will apply to the current and to the future.*

And that I think readers are leaders and people that are focused on those things that interest them. And in this case, we're talking about crisis management. So you would expect that people would be reading about what folks have done historically and there's so much documentation, you couldn't possibly read it in a lifetime in this space.

But I would say that is first and foremost is being an avid reader.

Number two, obviously, there's probably a lot of video entertainment that you could watch and learn lots of life lessons, and that's probably less relevant. But finally, having a mentor or someone that can provide you with a professional example of what leadership looks like. And you know, the difference between being a leader and a manager. The difference between being a leader and just being a figurehead.

You know, I've worked in organizations that were led by people that were not leaders, but they just happened to be there at the right time.

So, I guess those would be my thoughts about what to do if you really want to develop leadership skills is to *read a lot and find a great mentor.*

#5 - WHO IS A CRISIS LEADER THAT INFLUENCED YOUR CAREER?

A crisis leader that influenced my career.

This is, I guess, a little more difficult for me. I am a very avid reader. I'm a very avid reader of history. I'm very much a student of the civil war, so I really enjoy reading about what went on in the course of the war and leading up to the war.

In particular, I think you mentioned earlier someone talking about Lincoln, and Lincoln is my hero. But he's my all-time favorite historical figure because he saved the union, but he did it in a way that under today's standards he'd never make it to the White House, certainly. From Lincoln's example to this very day, if I see a politician who is an artistic orator, I immediately discount them as being a phony.

And I don't need to reference anyone in particular in our recent past but I firmly believe the guys that have difficulty in oration oftentimes are the ones that have that lack of hubris and that capability to think outwardly as opposed to inwardly, and maybe their skill set isn't all about reading from a prompter, but it's about *doing the right thing at the right time.*

So, when I think of great influencers, I think of guys that are just really great at getting the job done, and they're not about, as I said earlier, taking credit for it.

Anytime I see somebody that wants to be the guy at the front of the pack, I immediately discount them as being irrelevant.

KEY TAKEAWAYS

- Take the blame not the credit
- Common sense is a skillset
- Remain calm under pressure
- Ask "why?" Five times to figure out what is going on
- Readers are leaders
- Be an avid reader to learn lessons from the past
- Have a mentor to provide you a professional example of what leadership looks like
- Understand the difference between leaders and managers and leaders and figure-heads
- Do the right thing at the right time
- Have the discipline and foresight to reach out for other perspectives

WARREN "COUNTRY" WEIDLER –TX SAR COORDINATOR

Home	Austin, Texas
Then	Battalion Chief - Austin Fire Department
Now	Search & Rescue (SAR) Coordinator - State of Texas
Contact	**mailto:** cntryafd@yahoo.com
Quote	*"Calmness breeds calmness ..."*

WHY COUNTRY IS A CRISIS LEADER

The majority of people I interviewed for this project were selected because of my observations and insights about them after they made their name as a crisis leader.

I had never followed them into battle or benefit from their leadership first hand. I relied on the quality of their character to decide whether or not to request their involvement.

This interview is different because I've experienced Country's leadership first-hand on many occasions.

As an urban search and rescue disaster responder, "Country" was one of my leaders in 'battle,' and I have looked to him for guidance many times, even after our journeys took us in different directions.

As you'll see, his leadership style is on-point, direct, and effective.

And that pragmatic approach to crisis leadership is well suited for disaster response, too.

Early in my disaster response career, I was tasked to go on a mission that involved lots of moving parts and a fair amount of risk. My concern for those complexities overshadowed any confidence I had in my training to do the job, and Country detected that waning confidence.

He pulled me aside, put his arm around me and simply said: *"go do what you do, Mike, you've got this."*

And just like that, I was mentally fortified and ready to slay dragons.

It's been said that if you can't describe something simply, then you don't understand it very well.

That sentiment has never been truer than when listening to Country, particularly when he's in command-mode. He says in one sentence, what the rest of us may spend an hour to describe.

I've had the good fortune to serve under a few great leaders in my life, and Country is one of the best.

#1 - WHAT IS A CRISIS LEADER?

So what is a crisis leader?

My opinion and my version of a crisis leader is someone who is calming.

So whatever the situation is, you know it's not gonna get worse.

And it's that person's opportunity to make it better.

#2 - PLEASE SHARE AN EXAMPLE WHEN YOU RELIED ON YOUR CRISIS LEADERSHIP?

So, an example for me for crisis leadership.

There was an incident where a gentleman was mad at the IRS (Internal Revenue Service) and decided to fly his plane into that building. And, a lot of chaos, a lot of stuff there.

But I felt like when I showed up, things calmed down, and I took the time to gather good information. And, in the end, the death toll was minimal, but it could've been a lot worse.

But, we got there, took charge and calmed everything down.

It didn't change the fact that the fire was burning. It didn't change the fact that the building was destroyed, or there were deaths, but everything started kinda calm down, made better.

#3 - WHAT DO YOU KNOW NOW THAT YOU WISH YOU KNEW THEN?

Some of the things that I wished that I know now that I wish I knew before was to make sure you understand the *difference between a bad decision and a decision you don't want to make.*

Sometimes, things are just bad, but that doesn't change the fact that you still have to make the decision.

You don't like the decision, but you gotta make it anyway, and sometimes that gets confused. People confuse that with a bad decision, and it's not, it's just a decision that you wish you didn't have to make, and you just don't like it.

#4 - WHAT ADVICE WOULD YOU GIVE SOMEONE WHO WANTS TO IMPROVE THEIR CRISIS LEADERSHIP?

Some ways to improve your crisis leadership is you have to become a voracious reader.

You have got to read.

You must read about everybody else's crises.

And stuff that is not in your lane.

Read about the Ebola problem in Zaire.

Read about the water problem in Flint.

Read about the plastics problem in Argentina.

Whatever it is, I said go read, and you have to read and reread and look at some of those lessons.

NASA called them predictable surprises.

When you read it, I made it a point to always read at my fire service the line of duty death fatality reports. And as you're reading it, with the hindsight, you can see where it's gonna end.

Do the same thing with those other crises around the world, and different, I don't care if it's the Boeing 737 Max crisis; read about it.

There are things to learn, and that'll make you better.

#5 - WHO IS A CRISIS LEADER THAT INFLUENCED YOUR CAREER?

So, a crisis leader that had kinda inspired me, and look, there's a bunch I can read about.

338

Sullenberger did his thing; General Mattis did his things, there's all those you can read about.

But from a personal note, it's probably my father because we, and I say we, have always been accused of thinking outside of the box, but his version is he didn't know there was a box.

So he had never started that way.

And he worked for IBM, and he retired from there, but when there were problems, they always gave it to him to try to go solve. And he remembered that they weren't his problems, it's never your problem, and that you have to be, make decisions that make it better, not worse.

And he trusted his instinct, and he trusted his people, and he trusted his gut, very calm, doesn't get excited.

And *calmness breeds calmness*, so it's worked out well.

KEY TAKEAWAYS

o   Think outside the box
o   Never fail to make a decision
o   Read voraciously
o   Trust your instinct and your people

- Calmness breeds calmness
- Make the situation better, not worse
- Don't confuse bad decisions with decisions you don't want to make
- Read about other people's crises to learn how they solve them

ADDITIONAL RESOURCES

LEGACYOFLEADERSHIP.US

Visit the webpage to take advantage of the following items:

AUDIO AND VIDEO

Each interviewee has a dedicated page on my website where their interview is broken down by each question, with closed captioning and text transcription.

Future interviews and leadership legacy content will also be available, and access is limited to subscribers.

As a reader of this book, you may use code "*LOLBook20*" to access the videos.

KEY TAKEAWAY REPORT

An expanded report of the Key Takeaways from this book is also available for downloading and printing.

After reading each interview, I interpreted and documented a total of **242 Key Takeaways**.

I evaluated each Key Takeaway and developed a list of **12 priority themes** across all 242 Key Takeaways using 479 data points.

In addition to sharing all of the Key Takeaways in one place, I ranked each priority theme by usage and applicability.

"Learn Continuously," for example, is a priority theme that occurs in 95% of the interviews.

The data and the resulting report will be updated as I index more and more crisis leaders and their answers.

Armed with the results of these often unspoken priorities, we're able to plan and build a rock-solid legacy of our own.

This exclusive and one-of-a-kind report is only available at LegacyOfLeadership.US.

CURRENT OR EMERGING LEADER?

Are you a current or emerging leader and want to contribute to Volume 2 of this ongoing Leadership Legacy project?

Please contact me at LegacyOfLeadership.US and tell me your crisis leadership stories!

Mike.

Made in the USA
Monee, IL
23 November 2019